WHERE WAS GOD?

A Raw and Unedited Memoir

By:Jennifer Dawn Turpin

Cover by JR Taylor

TABLE OF CONTENTS

Introduction

1. Younger Years
2. Tortured
3. Heartless
4. Hope
5. Abandoned
6. Dealing With Suicide
7. My Escape
8. California
9. Starved
10. What Got Me Through
11. Spreading God's Word
12. Animal Cruelty
13. This Is It
14. Surrender From War
15. Rescued
16. My Statement
17. My Life Now

Conclusion

INTRODUCTION

Have you heard about the "Turpin 13" and wondered what actually happened. I am Jennifer Turpin. I'm the oldest of the Turpin 13 children. This is my story through my eyes, through my perspective. Just like any story there is more than one side. To this story there are 15 sides. Yes, we all lived in the same house most of the time. But we were all fighting our own battles. And some things were done behind closed doors. Warning! This may be very triggering for some people. I went through hell, but I wouldn't change my past. It made me who I am today. It's also how I found God. He was my only hope.

You're probably wondering why I named this book "Where Was God?". It is my hope that by the end of this book, it will be explained. A lot of people who go through extreme situations ask "Where was God when I needed Him most?" Or "If He's real why didn't he save me?". There were many times I felt like He wasn't there, felt like He didn't care. But, I would hold onto what the Bible said, "He will never leave or forsake you" "Walk by faith, not by sight". It was very hard to keep my faith. But, God was my only hope, so I chose to hold onto Him. And, each time my faith would only strengthen. I hope you enjoy my story. Just remember it's not the full story, just 1 out of 15 stories.

I would suggest reading a little at a time. I would not recommend reading it all at once. This book gets deep and dark. It may very likely trigger anything from your past. But even if you're completely ok and nothing like that will be triggered, you could have some unpleasant nightmares.

Read at your own pace. I include topics on mental, physical, and emotional abuse. I talk about suicidal thoughts and why I wanted to just end it all. So, yes, it can be very triggering. So, please read with caution. There's some things I've left out on purpose. Either I'm not ready to share or I never will be.

I know that this book is not grammatically correct and probably needs lots of editing. I wrote it this way so everyone can see my level of education. My education is technically only up to the 3rd grade level. Almost everything else I taught myself. This book may not flow as well as the books you're used to reading.

1. YOUNGER YEARS

My life wasn't always hell. I had a fairly normal childhood in Texas until I was 11. I had a caring and loving mother, I went to school and made friends, I visited family, I was taught about Jesus, and I went to church every Sunday.

Every summer or winter, sometimes both, we'd visit family that lived in West Virginia. We'd visit grandparents, great grandparents, aunts, uncles, cousins, and other family members that I don't remember how we're related. One summer my paternal grandfather taught me how to swing. Everytime I swing, I think of that and smile.

My favorite memory out there was our last winter at my paternal grandparents home. It was my first and last time playing in snow. I made snow angels, built a snowman, made footprints purposely, and made snowballs to throw at nothing. My hands may have been numb from the snow, but I loved every second of it. I loved going to West Virginia, especially in the winter time. The snow is so beautiful! I couldn't wait to go back and do it all over again. I had no idea that would also be my last time.

Another really good memory was one summer. I was allowed to go in my maternal grandfather's backyard and catch lightning bugs at night. They're also known as fireflies. They're such cool bugs and it was so cool seeing them all come out at night.

There was a time when my mother was caring. She would tuck me into bed every night and read me a bedtime story. She would allow me to crawl into her bed if I got afraid of monsters being in my room. I rarely saw her angry. We'd watch TV shows together. My favorite thing we watched was a pastor. At the end he'd put his hands up to pray with those watching at home. My mother would put one hand on his, and I'd put one hand on his other. We'd bow our heads in prayer with him. We'd also watch game shows and try to guess all the answers.

When I was 4, I was told about God and Jesus. I was told and explained The Ten Commandments. I was also told how God made us, and Jesus came to earth to save us from our sins. I kind of already knew, because of church. I prayed for forgiveness for the first time, but I was just a child and didn't really know what I was doing.

A really good memory and really good advice I have from my mother was about the Bible. I had just learned to read. I believe I was 7 years old. I had started reading Genesis, and had a question. I don't remember what it was but something had confused me. I went downstairs to ask my mother about it. She told me that if I have any questions about the Bible to pray and ask God. That advice I used starting from when I was 16.

We used to celebrate Halloween. Each year we'd dress up and go trick or treating. I remember getting lots of candy. I was 9 the last time we went trick or treating.

I never believed in Santa, the Easter Bunny, or anything like that except for the tooth fairy. I did believe in her. Until one day, when I was 7, I decided to test it. I thought if the others aren't real, she might not be either. I had lost my tooth at school, and decided not to tell anyone. That night I put the tooth under my pillow. I woke up the next morning and my tooth was still there, no money. I was pretty disappointed. I decided to keep it a secret that I found out the truth. I pretended I had just lost it. I told my parents and that night put it under my pillow. The next morning when I looked under my pillow, the tooth was gone and there was money in its place. I continued to pretend to believe in the tooth fairy, so I'd still receive money.

I wasn't trapped when I was younger. I did get to go out and do things. From as far back as I can remember until I was about 8, I had been sent to daycare quite a bit. I loved playing with the other children. I didn't love nap time though. I also went to a public school up to the 3rd grade. I made a friend here and there, but they'd only be around for one school year or less. I did make what I feel like would've been 3 long term friends if I had stayed in school. One of them I helped a lot, one of them I stood up for, and one of them I was friends with for 2 years.

When I was in kindergarten, my teacher asked me what I wanted to be when I grew up. I seriously thought about it. I knew I wanted to be a singer, but I also knew I wanted to help people. My little mind didn't know that singers could help people with their music. I only knew of 3 things that helped people; doctors, fire fighters, and the police. I thought all police officers died and I didn't want to die. I also didn't want to walk through fire. So that left me with a doctor or a singer. At 5 years old I chose a doctor over what I thought I'd enjoy more because I wanted to help others. Somehow that's always been a desire of mine. Throughout the years my desire to help others only grew.

From 1st to 3rd grade, I played soccer. I loved it so much and played every day possible. I was really good at it, or I thought I was, though I wasn't much of a team player. I would get the ball and basically play defense the entire way to the goal. I kicked and blocked and always made it to the goal. We won almost every game, so I didn't know why my team was so mad at me. They were wanting me to pass the ball to them and give them a chance to play. I thought if I passed the ball that we'd lose the ball. One time, I did pass it to a teammate just to make them happy. And sure enough the opposite team got the ball instead of my teammate, and we lost that game. I never passed it again. When I started 3rd grade, the gym instructors placed me as the goalie. I was a little sad at first. They explained that they only place the best players as the goalie. Now that I'm older I think it was really because I wasn't playing as a team. After playing as a goalie for a few weeks, I actually enjoyed it. Our team still won more than lost. It was like 60% of the games we won. I really miss playing soccer.

We also went to church every Sunday. I got to be a part of a Christmas play there when I was 9. It was so much fun learning the parts and all the music. One day the instructor asked me to come into her office. There she told me that I have a very beautiful voice and she wanted to give me a solo. I was so honored and happy. She was the 2nd person to complement my voice. My mother was the first.

When I was 4, I was singing in my room to my cassette player. My mother called for me. When I saw her she asked if I was singing. I told her I was. She then told me that I sing really good, and that the wavy thing I do with my voice, only very talented people can do. Not long after, they bought me a standing microphone. They would take videos of me singing.

Another thing I did at church that I loved was making strawberry jam. It was a Wednesday night. Me and some other girls around my age were making strawberry jam. It was so much fun. I had watched my mother cook in the kitchen and wished I could help her. After making the jam, I wanted to help in the kitchen even more but wasn't allowed to.

When I was 10, I was pulled from school and started being homeschooled. They pulled me because my 3rd grade teacher wasn't teaching me anything. And if I got an F, she'd give me a picture to color. Then she'd raise my grade. Well, that's what I was told anyway. When homeschooled I was being taught everyday Monday through Friday. It was actually kind of fun, and I didn't have to get up early. I did really miss my friends though. I had no way to contact them.

Even though I had these good times during my childhood, I also had bad times. I did have a caring but not perfect mother, but I always remember my father being abusive. He wasn't toward me yet, but he was toward my mother.

My first vivid memory is when I was either 2 or 3 years old. I was going down the stairs to ask for some water. I stopped halfway down them because for the first time I saw my parents fighting, more like just my father doing the fighting. I stood frozen with fear as he was yelling very loudly. When my mother tried to speak up, he yelled for her to shut up. She did. He punched a hole in the wall with his fist. At that moment I ran up to my room as fast as I could. I laid on my bed and cried myself to sleep. When I woke up, I ran downstairs to check on my mother. I wanted to make sure she was alive. I don't know how I knew about death at such a young age. When I reached the bottom of the stairs, I saw her in the living room. I gave her a big hug. I was so happy to see she was ok.

Growing up I saw things like that a lot. I'd see him yell and not let her speak during fights. I'd see him hit, choke, and push her down into the floor. I'd also see him throw things at her like soda pop bottles, cans, and random things he'd see on the floor.

My mother did have her bad side when I was little. When we'd be at the store sometimes I would start looking at a toy or even beg for one. I'd also like to dance to the music that the store would be playing. When I did these and other little things, my mother would grab my arm hard enough to leave deep pinch marks and sometimes bleed. She had really long nails. I'd make a face because it hurt really bad. She'd say, "Don't overreact.", "You're making a scene.", and things like that. I would have to wear long sleeves to cover the marks up. When I did wear short sleeves I was told I better keep my arms down. I had scars from that for many years. I noticed they were fading and almost gone when I was 18 years old.

School was good but also bad. The other kids made fun of my size and stench. The stench was from filth that I had to live in. I would get laughed at and called names. 2 girls would do whatever they could to turn other kids and new kids against me and to laugh at me. I did my best not to let it get to me. I kept a positive attitude. This went on from 1st to 3rd grade.

From kindergarten to 3rd grade it was very hard to stay sitting in one place. I would get in trouble for getting up, dancing, or singing. I would try not to get restless during class time, but it was very hard. Even to this day I get restless if I sit down for too long. I have learned that it's a part of my ADHD.

Because of me not being able to "behave" I had to go to an inbetween school after kindergarten. I was told I wasn't mature enough to go to first grade. The grade was called D-1. One day at lunch a girl, probably in her teens, asked me to help her get her medicine. I have always been willing to help others. So, I said I would. I was a little confused why she couldn't get it herself. She led me to her classroom, and had me go inside. It was dark. I found her backpack hanging where she said it would be. Someone walked inside the classroom and caught me by her backpack. I was sent to the principal's office and then sent home. I got in so much trouble and did not understand. I thought it was good to help others.

Now that I'm older and know a lot more. I think she probably had drugs in that backpack, and had me get it so I'd be the one caught instead of her. That would definitely explain why I got into so much trouble for it.

Practically my entire life I have lived in filth and flies, lots of flies. When the place was cleaned up, it'd get piled and filthy soon after. By filth I mean trash piled anywhere from ankle to knee deep all over the house, mold on the floor and walls, and lots of flies and maggots. When we were going to have visitors, we'd have to clean up everything at the last minute. It was always last minute. And I did most of the cleaning. I think the worst part was scratching the mold off of the floor.

I was accused of lying about foods I liked and foods I didn't like. Why would I even want to do that? Some things I loved but was accused of not liking were cheesecake and lemon tea. And some things I didn't like at all but was accused of liking were green beans, jello, and those kid TV dinners. I was made to eat what they thought I liked, it didn't matter what I said. Why would I want to miss out on something I liked? I'm not going to lie about that.

The thing that I was accused of not liking that bothered me most was green beans. My parents would say that I had to be lying. That I must like them because they've loved them their entire life. But when I was about 7 and my sister said she didn't like them, they believed her. My mother told my sister that she didn't like them when she was little and they understand her not liking them. They did have her eat green beans anyway. But I was left feeling confused and upset. They told me and her something completely differently.

I have an aunt who, on public television, told a story about her living with us. Her story wasn't completely true. Here's my side of the story. We went to West Virginia to visit family. She asked to come with us to Texas, I don't know the reason. She lived with us for a little while. My mother was in the hospital giving birth to one of my siblings. My aunt was supposed to be babysitting us. My father called to check and see how we were doing. While on the phone, my aunt yelled at my brother who was maybe 4 years old to get a rag. Because she yelled and it sounded angrily, she was kicked out.

I wanted to tell this story because it shows I did have somewhat of a decent childhood, but I also watched my whole childhood rip away from me when I was 11 years old. I watched everything disappear and become a living total nightmare.

When I was 11 my entire life changed. We moved to a country area. I was excited about the move. I had no memory of moving before. But right after the move I noticed my mother changing. She started getting angry easily and started disciplining out of anger instead of disciplining out of love.

We also stopped visiting family. Most contact was cut off due to fear of them calling CPS. My parents made CPS sound bad. They said we'd be all split up across the United States. That we'd have no contact with each other. And that CPS would make sure of that. That anyone over 18 would go to jail where we'd be beat and raped, or we'd be homeless. They said CPS loves pulling children away from their parents and that our lives would be miserable. So the family that couldn't know about the filth, lack of education, and abuse they shut out. My mother's mom and her two sisters were still in communication.

We had just moved and like way too much I heard my father yelling at my mother. I was in the living room and they were in the master bedroom. I heard my mother yell, "No, I will NOT be quiet!" I thought that was good, I thought maybe things were going to change for the better. I was wrong. With her new found voice, she started using it on us. If something made her angry, even a little, she'd yell at us. She also started hitting us out of anger. She had reached her breaking point of being abused and she snapped.

She used to, before she snapped, when I did something wrong she'd sit down and tell me what I did and why it was wrong. Then she'd discipline out of love. But now at this point, she got angry and would hit me or discipline me on the spot. She disciplined out of anger. I remember telling 2 of my siblings, quite often, "Mommy's changing." I started saying that only about one week after moving in.

When I was little I called my parents Mommy and Daddy. After things started changing I was told to start calling them Mother and Father. They said it is more respectful because that's what the Bible uses.

I started getting stuff I wasn't allowed to. It started with getting my parents' cheesecake bars. One taste and I was hooked. I would also get cans and bottles of lemon tea. I would crave the food and drinks I supposedly didn't like. I started getting other food, snacks, and drinks without permission. I would lie out of fear of being caught. Whether I got it or one of my siblings got it, it didn't matter. I got blamed unless I proved someone else did it. My siblings knew that and took advantage. Now, remember they were just children. Anything they did, I do not hold against them.

I was 11 when I took my first shower instead of a bath. No one warned me about the floor being slippery. When I cleaned my feet and I put my soapy foot on the floor of the tub, I slipped and blacked out. I have no idea how long I was laying there. When I woke up, I knew nothing. I can't explain it, but I had no memory at all. I was just laying there in the water looking around, not even acknowledging that I was wet from the water. After a while my memory was slowly coming back. First I realized I was wet, then that the water was pouring on me. Then I realized I was in a bathroom. Then I remembered I was taking a bath, and all my memory flooded back. I jumped up in fear. How long was I out? How long was I even laying there with no memory? Was it long enough for my parents to be angry with me? I turned the water off and got out as fast as I could. Thankfully they didn't act like I took too long. I never told them about it out of fear of not being believed.

While homeschooling she got really angry if I didn't know the answer. She'd say things like, "you're ___ years old! Most kids ___ years old know this!" She'd call me stupid for not knowing an answer. At the beginning she would help me. After she changed I didn't receive help. I was expected to automatically know the answer. It made it harder to focus with her yelling and hitting me. I have a scar on my right hand from "not knowing an answer". I was doing some math flash cards. I didn't know an answer fast enough so she ripped a plastic headband off my head and hit my hand hard enough for it to break the headband in two and make a pretty big cut on my hand. She didn't apologize, she was so angry with me.

She slacked off of teaching us. She would stop, wait a year or more, then start us in a new grade. My parents had started me in 3rd grade work and some 4th. So I did quite a bit in those grades. But then everything changed. I did about 20 lessons in 5th grade, 3-5 in 6th, 30 in 7th, and none in 8th-12th. The subjects were Reading, Math, English, and Spelling.

I know this book might not always be grammatically correct and it might not flow as well as what you're used to reading, but I take pride in that due to my education level. I wasn't learning anything jumping from grade to grade and only a few lessons in each.

Extreme punishments started happening. I remember clearly my first extreme beating. I was 11. My parents handcuffed me to the leg of my bed. My father pulled my pants off and beat me with a tree branch. He was hitting me very hard. It was too hard to lay still. He said he wouldn't stop beating me until I lay still. He decided to sit on my lower legs to hold me still. I bled from that beating but they didn't care. Afterwards, he poured rubbing alcohol on it.

Not long after we moved our aunt, uncle, and cousins came to visit. It's the same aunt I had mentioned earlier. She was now married and had children. My parents gave her husband the paddle and had him spank me for no reason at all. Her husband said it was an honor. The aunt stood there smiling. When I asked my mother why I was getting the paddling, she said, "There's always a reason for you to be punished." After that, I spent as much time in my room as I could to avoid seeing my aunt or my uncle.

One day, my brother wanted his train set off his bedroom shelf. I stood on the toy box to reach for it. I managed to get a track piece down and turned around to hand it to my brother. When I turned I saw my father standing there looking very angry. I was terrified. This was the first time I saw him angry at someone other than my mother. He picked me up and slammed me against the wall. He was yelling at me asking what I thought I was doing and calling me the devil. He yelled many things, but I don't remember what else he said. This was also the first of many times he slammed me against the wall, my feet off the floor. I was so afraid and confused. I still don't know what I did wrong.

That was the beginning of a lifetime of Hell. I had lost everything. My father took everything away from me. My childhood, my happiness, my mother. And yes, my mother is very much responsible for her actions. But I feel like he did take her away from me.

2. TORTURED

From 11-15 years old, I was in complete torture. The only word I know to explain it is hell. Instead of my father abusing my mother as much, they were both abusing me. I was slapped for just smiling. My happiness made my parents angry, or it sure seemed like it. I was in constant punishment even when I hadn't done anything. Also we were living in knee high to ankle high trash, mice, snakes, and many different kinds of bugs.

I was taught that taking stuff that isn't yours is stealing. So, everything I craved and got was stealing. I wanted to stop after finding out I was sinning. But at that point I was basically addicted. It seemed that no matter how hard I tried to stop, it was impossible. I saw food of my parents that I knew I couldn't ever have, and I craved it badly. It didn't help that most of my cravings were from things I "didn't" like. So, I took it.

From my understanding, I almost died at the age of 14. I believe God saved me from dying. I will tell the story in another chapter. After that I started trying much harder to stop stealing and lying. Again, I was addicted, so it was a total struggle. Everytime I stopped, I'd start again. Each time I felt bad but just kept trying to stop. And, I lied about getting it because I feared what would happen to me.

When I was 12, I started having to watch my siblings when my parents would leave. That just added to the stressful life I already had. I will also talk about this more in detail in another chapter. Watching my siblings meant staying home all the time, very rarely going out. I wasn't able to go to the bathroom, because when I did I always got in trouble for something. I felt like I was going to go crazy. It wasn't all bad though. I made the best of the situation. It was the one time I was allowed to look away from the door or wall, to play or talk to my siblings, and to be away from my parents' cruelty.

Between the ages of 12 and 15, I was constantly in a time out. Most of the time, staring at a door or wall not able to mess with anything. I was bored, once I got something given to me, it was taken away soon after. Because of that, I got creative, and learned that if I really wanted something like playing cards I could make it. I also learned that you can make almost anything out of paper. Pretty much the only time I was allowed to move was when I had to watch my siblings.

When I was 12, I tried to surprise my mother and clean the living room. I thought for sure she'd be happy and take me out of my time out stage. All I wanted was to make her proud of me. My parents had left to go to the store, so I started cleaning. I filled store plastic bags, tied them up, and put them against the wall. I got most of the living room clean by the time they came home. But their reaction was the opposite of what I expected. I was sure this would've made my mother happy. Instead she got angry and yelled at me. She made me dump each bag out and back onto the floor. I was so confused, but mostly hurt. I told her I did it for her, but she didn't care. I vowed that would be the last time I ever tried to surprise her.

I would try to teach my younger siblings how to read and some math. Any time I was caught, I got punished. I was told, "that's my job" by my mother. Well, if it's her job then why didn't she do it! I still continued to sneak and teach what I could.

From 12 to 13 years old, all I was given to eat were peanut butter sandwiches as a punishment. I hated the sandwiches. The more I ate, the more nasty it was to me. I started secretly hiding them in the trash on the floor.

I was beaten with the belt, the buckle of the belt, branches, and a rod made of fiberglass from a miniature ball pit. I was usually beat until I bled and then some. Then they'd laugh as they poured rubbing alcohol on it. I have a big scar on my right hip from the rod they used.

One night I was sleeping, and I woke up to my father beating me with his belt on my bare legs. They were both laughing. I was afraid but I fell asleep after he stopped. I woke up again, he was beating me again. They were laughing again. I tried to stay awake, but I fell asleep again. And, I woke up to the same thing again.

I had a cat named Smokey. She was my first real pet. I took care of her and loved her with all my heart. She made me happy during all this darkness. I stole some apple juice, and lied about it. Because of that I had to carry Smokey to her death. I will share the entire story in the next chapter.

For a punishment me and 2 of my siblings were literally starved for 3 whole days. We were watched extra closely to make sure we didn't steal anything. The only thing we were allowed to drink was the shower water, it was the only thing we were allowed at all. It had stuff floating in it, and tasted awful.

When I was 12, I was locked outside at night. We had coyotes that would come out at night. I was scared and crying. I said to my mother, "What if the coyotes attack me?" She just replied, "One less thing to worry about." I knew what she meant by that. I was left out there for about 2 hours, I think. I could hear the howling. I do not know or remember why she locked me out there.

I would have to carry way too heavy to lift black trash bags from the master bedroom, through the kitchen, through the hall, and into the living room. At this time the living room was basically a giant dumpster. It was dark because the lights were burnt out and I usually had to do this at night. There were snakes, mice, and big spiders everywhere. We had poisonous and non-poisonous snakes and spiders. I've been the one mostly responsible for cleaning the trash piled houses from the age 5 or 6 to 21 when needed for someone coming over or us moving.

I was the one to bring things to my parents and do most of the food preparation from the age 12 to 21, then it was mostly me but sometimes a couple other siblings till I was 29 and rescued. I would see and smell their yummy food, making me want it so bad. My parents would sit and watch television while I made their food. I would get accused of cooking it wrong when the microwave wasn't working. And if I had even a very simple question about how to fix the food, I'd get knocked and hit on the head and I'd get yelled at. I felt like a slave. I felt like I was only there to cook, clean when asked, and to babysit my siblings. I felt unloved by the people who were supposed to love me unconditionally.

When I was 12, I was told to clean up in the master bedroom. I was afraid because of the snakes in there. But that didn't matter to my parents. They made me do it anyway. When I started cleaning under the bed something horrific happened, to me it was horrific. I reached my hand under the bed, and felt something really weird. When I pulled my hand out from under it, my hand was completely covered in little spiders! I was too scared to move. None of them bit me, probably because I sat so still. They slowly spun a string of web to get off my hand and onto the floor. After they were all off I ran as fast as I could out of that room. I refused to go back and clean. Of course I got punished and according to my parents I was "over exaggerating", but there was no way I was cleaning under that bed again. From then until I was 25 I had a crazy huge fear of spiders. I couldn't even see a still picture of one or hear someone talk about them. I freaked out every time. The fear just got worse and worse.

When I was 24, we went to the zoo. In an aquarium they had a beautiful orange tarantula. My mother literally pushed me to the aquarium. I was crying and telling her no the entire time. She just got angry and told me to stop causing a scene. She was the one causing the scene! She was only making things worse for me, not helping!

She was constantly telling me that I was crazy, that something was wrong with me, that I'm just being stupid, that I'm overreacting, that no one is that scared of anything. I started believing that I was actually crazy and stupid. But the fear was real, very real. I was not overreacting at all.

When I was 25, one of my brothers downloaded a realistic spider app where you care for virtual tarantulas. I couldn't stand watching him play it. But, after a while I realized that might be a good way to try to overcome the crazy fear, or at least the "crazy" part. I prayed and asked for God's help and strength.

It was one of the hardest things I've done. I downloaded it and started forcing myself to care for the virtual tarantulas. It was complete torture! Everytime I closed my eyes I saw a giant tarantula. Every dream was a nightmare filled with all kinds of spiders. I would feel them on me when I was awake, but nothing was there. I kept wanting to delete it, but wanted more not to be crazy anymore. Besides, I felt like if I stopped then all the torture would've been for nothing. So, I pushed through. After about a month the nightmares and everything else calmed down and almost went completely away. The app didn't really bother me anymore. So I deleted the app because my phone needed the storage space. Then I put everything I did to the test. Did it work? Or was it all for nothing?

I watched a movie I said I never would. It was about a guy who shrinks and shrinks. In one scene he comes face to face with a spider much bigger than him. I was afraid for that scene, but I was so relieved when it came. The scene did not bother me! I was so happy! I wasn't crazy anymore. There was no way I could even look at a still picture before. Next, was the real test.

I believe I was still 25, we went back to the zoo. I asked to go see the orange tarantula I saw before. I walked over to it on my own. I was not afraid, but in the back of my mind I felt like turning around to run. When I reached the aquarium, I touched the glass right where the tarantula was. I cried! I wasn't afraid! I was so happy!

I had this fear for 13 years, and then it was gone! Now, my only fear is, what if it returns? Spiders still creep me out sometimes, but at least that's normal. I am so glad I don't have to be tortured by them anymore.

One day while I was microwaving TV dinners for everyone, I saw a really big snake. It was about 3 inches in diameter. I was terrified and about 13 years old. I ran into the bedroom to tell my parents about the snake. They started telling me the story of the little boy who cried wolf. They didn't believe me. I had never nor would I ever lie about something like that. I insisted that my story was true. My father went into the kitchen, but he didn't see it. They were more sure I was lying. So, I went back into the kitchen and saw it again. It was in a different place. I ran back into the bedroom, refusing to go back into the kitchen. My father went again. This time he saw it, so they knew I wasn't lying. But then he got his gun and shot it. I felt horrible for the snake.

I had to ask before going to the bathroom each time. Most of the time I was told to hold it. It didn't matter how bad I had to go. There were times I could not hold it or was afraid to ask. So, I would urinate in the trash, in a bucket, in a cup, or in a diaper. When I told them I couldn't hold it, I really couldn't.

I have had several episodes when I urinated in my sleep. I tried to help it, but I couldn't. My parents would say, "Look at the baby!" in front of my siblings. At 12-14, I was made to wear diapers and a shirt. My mother literally laid me on the bed and put them on me. When I was 14, I saw pinworms in my stool. I showed my mother. They bought pinworm medicine for all of us. I later saw a paper from the medicine on the floor. I picked it up and read it. One of the symptoms of having pinworms is uncontrolled urination. I have had pinworms a total of 5 times. Twice they were gone by medicine, and 3 times they were gone by faith that God would take them away.

I used to draw a lot! I knew I didn't draw well, but I did my best. When I was about 13, I showed my parents a picture of a bear I drew, and they literally made fun of it. They pointed at the flawed parts and laughed. They said bears don't stand up like that, that they stand up on all fours. Then they showed my siblings while still laughing at it. I stopped drawing after that. I didn't try drawing again until I was 16. And I kept my drawings secret until I was 20. By the time I was 20, I didn't care if they thought my drawings were stupid.

When I was 14, I had lost my Christmas because I stole some cough drops. I had a cold, and medicine wasn't much of a necessity according to my mother. So, I found a pack of expired cough drops to make me feel better. It didn't matter how I felt or if I was sick, I was still made to do everything as though I was healthy. So, I took the cough drops to try to help me. I lost all my presents, and had to watch everyone else open theirs. I also watched as my presents were opened by my mother. Then they played a song about getting nothing for Christmas. It used to be one of my favorite Christmas songs to sing as a child. Now, I hate it because of this moment. They had the song on repeat. They sang it directly to me, "You're getting nothing for Christmas". Then they had my siblings sing it that way. Then my father held the belt, ready to hit me in the head with the buckle of his belt. I was made to sing the song or I was going to get hit.

Several times I was accused of trying to kill my siblings, accused of not loving them. 2 moments that were brought up too often was when I was about 4 and when I was about 14. Neither one makes sense to me, and why would I try to kill them. I LOVED them! I honestly think it was brought up just to hurt me.

When I was about 4, I had given baby flu medicine to my baby brother. Yes, it was dangerous, but I was trying to take care of him. I definitely wasn't trying to hurt him. I saw my mother do it, and thought I was helping. The medicine should've been out of reach for a child. I shouldn't have been able to get it in the first place.

When I was about 14, I helped my siblings sneak out the bathroom window while my parents were gone to the store. We played outside for quite a while. Then we tried to rush back into the house when I noticed my parents coming home. They knew we had been outside. I got accused of trying to kill them because of the snakes. Now, that was stupid because we were living in nests of snakes and mice, in our house! It was most likely safer outside!

By my mother, I was pushed literally across the room and yanked by my hair across the room. I was hit with a bottle or her knuckles on my head causing a headache. I was slapped for just smiling, pinched with long nails and made to bleed, accused of not loving my parents or siblings, said when I die, I'm going exactly where I belong-Hell, and many other hurtful things. I was told that I never loved her, that hurt so much. I was constantly called Lucifer. Lucifer sounds like Jennifer, so I started hating my name. I was told that if I dropped dead, everyone would sing and dance around me. That everyone would be happier and better off if I was dead. She said stuff like these things to me constantly.

By my father, I was beaten till I bled, literally picked up and thrown across the room, slammed against the wall while being yelled at, thrown and pinned on the floor while being yelled at, and was choked and couldn't breathe. The only thing that saved me is, when I would be choked my mother would beg him to stop.

They both would constantly bring up scriptures from the Bible to back up their behavior. Their favorite to bring up was in Deuteronomy. Parents brought their rebellious son to the leaders. The leaders killed him. My parents would say that according to that they have the right to kill me, and that I should have already been killed. Thankfully I knew not to believe that God would be ok with them killing me. In the old testament everything was much different. What they did to that son was like what they call today the death penalty. If my parents had killed me that's where they would've gone, the death penalty. And I believe I'd be in Heaven.

With all this torture, I don't know how I mentally survived. But thanks to God I did. I believe He made me smart enough to be strong and not let them change me or completely damage my mind.

3. HEARTLESS

This chapter is three heartless stories. The first one my parents did something very heartless and evil. The second story I did something heartless. And the third story is about me almost changing and about the fight to not become a monster like them.

1-Smokey (Parents Being Heartless)

When I was 11, I was told to go outside to bring some soda pop from our van into the house. At the time things were still transitioning into the tortured life I would soon know.

I went out there and noticed our dogs barking like crazy. We had about 5 dogs. I looked over to see what they were barking at. There was a grey cat up in a tree. It looked at me and meowed. I began calling the dogs but they would not listen. I didn't know much I could do to help the cat, so I proceeded with getting the soda pop out of the van.

I went over to the house door. As soon as I opened the screen door the cat zoomed out of the tree and in between both doors. The dogs were trying so hard to get the cat. I just kept kicking them away and calling them bad dogs. The cat looked calm, but just stared at me the entire time. I was sure she knew I was keeping her safe.

I couldn't go inside the house because I knew I would've been in huge trouble for the cat running in. I also knew I could get in trouble for just standing there. I decided waiting was the best choice. And, I figured someone would come looking for me eventually.

After what seemed like forever, but probably less than an hour, my mother came to the door with an angry face. Before she opened the door I pointed to the cat and said, "There's a cat right here." My mother looked down and slowly opened the door. To my surprise she wasn't mad at me. She picked the cat up and brought her into the house.

My parents discussed what to do with the cat. I was in another room and couldn't hear anything. After a while they told me they were going to let me keep her. I was so happy! This was my first actual pet. The first one I got to care for. They said she had to stay in the bathroom.

They put her in the bathroom and we went to the store. My parents bought cat food, litter, a litter box, litter box liners, a scoop, and a water and food bowl.

When we got home we discussed names. Several were mentioned, but when the name Smokey was mentioned I knew that was perfect. I was shown how and when to change the litter and feed her.

I took care of her every day. Every chance I got, I played with her. I kept her well fed and she had a ton of love. She gave me so much joy and light, especially the worse things got.

When I would shower, she'd walk along the edge of the bathtub until I got out. Once she jumped into the shower while the water was on. She jumped out super fast and never tried that again. She would also drink water straight from the faucet, and she loved to hide in the cabinets.

About a year after I was told I could keep her, things were completely torture. Smokey brought me happiness, laughter, and light. She was my best friend.

When I was 12, I had stolen a bottle of my parents' apple juice. I was thirsty and all we were allowed to drink was the nasty shower water. I was also craving something cold. The shower water was warm. When it was noticed missing I was automatically accused of getting it. I lied and said I didn't get it, out of fear. For my punishment I was told I had to carry Smokey outside. I said, "No! The dogs will kill her!" My mother said, "Not my problem."

My father held the belt ready to hit me in the head with the buckle if I didn't do as asked. They both followed me to the bathroom. I picked up Smokey. I cried and held her tight all the way to the front door. I put Smokey down outside and ran into the kitchen crying. I don't know where my father went, maybe outside. My mother stood outside.

After a while, I have no idea how much time passed, my mother told me to come outside. I refused and was pushed outside. I saw Smokey trapped into a corner. Our dogs were attacking her. She looked up at me and meowed for help. I yanked my arm out of my mother's hand and ran back into the kitchen crying.

The next morning, my mother told me they saw Smokey's bones scattered. For some reason both my mother and father found that funny. In that moment I literally hated them, pure hate. That was one of the most evil things they've done!

When I was about 28, my mother and father told me that they were sorry for what they did to Smokey. But they also said that they would've gotten rid of her no matter what. That I just gave them the perfect excuse when I lied. Umm that's supposed to make me feel better?! How?! That just told me that this was planned for who knows how long.

2-My Throat (Me Being Heartless)

After I had been watching my siblings for about a year or two, my parents seemed to leave more often. Sometimes they'd be gone all night. I wasn't allowed to go to sleep until all of my siblings were asleep.

When I was 14, I was pretending to smoke using the back end of a plastic knife. I wasn't allowed to pretend to smoke at all. I got in trouble whenever I was caught. But, my parents were gone and I tried to get away with it.

The knife slipped and stabbed the back of my throat. I could feel gushes of blood rushing in the back of my throat. My parents came home not long after. I showed them my throat. They looked really scared and asked me what happened. I lied. I told them one of my siblings did it with the back end of a plastic spoon. I told them the sibling was angry, and my parents believed me. That sibling was already known for hurting us randomly, and out of fear I used that to my advantage.

There is no reason or excuse to pin something like this on anyone, especially a sibling. I lied because I was afraid of getting in trouble for pretending to smoke. I continued to stick to my lie out of fear of what would happen to me for lying. My sibling got a small spanking for stabbing me in the throat. If I had told the truth, I would've been beaten until I bled for pretending to smoke.

My parents told me the wound was literally gushing blood, and they didn't know if I'd live. I felt very lightheaded at that thought. They had me gargle mouthwash quite a lot. My throat began feeling numb. I don't know how many days passed doing that and only eating pudding and drinking weight loss meal substitute shakes.

I was told that my throat healed perfectly. My parents told me it was a miracle, It didn't leave a scar. I couldn't help but wonder if God had saved me. But, why? I mean I did blame it on my sibling, he got spanked for it, I never came clean about it, and I wasn't allowed to pretend to smoke. To this day I haven't told my parents the truth about it. I came clean to my sibling after we were rescued. My sibling had actually started believing they had done it. That made me feel so much worse about it.

I tried so much harder to stop stealing and lying about what I stole. But like I mentioned in an earlier chapter, it had become like an addiction. It felt impossible to stop getting the foods and drinks I craved. From then I just kept trying and slipping, but definitely trying.

3-They Almost Changed Me (Me Coming Close To Becoming A Monster Like My Parents)

I almost let my parents change me like my father changed my mother. It was a constant battle to not let that happen. It all started when I was 12. I was made to watch 5 of my siblings when my parents left the house. I was too young to have the sudden responsibility of 5 children.

My siblings being children, ranging from 8-1 years old, they knew I would get in trouble for anything they did. My parents would say that right in front of my siblings. Being children they took advantage of that. They did anything they wanted and didn't listen to me because I wasn't "Mother".

So, I had the stress of everything going on with my parents, plus I had the stress of my siblings not listening and getting me in trouble. I started taking my anger and stress out on my siblings. I would hit them, pinch them, yell at them, and push them for not listening to me even if it was something small. The range would be from getting into something important of my parents to not sitting where I told them to.

When I was 15, I realized I was following into what my mother had done. I was letting them change me like my father changed my mother. I was not about to let them change me into a monster too. What I was doing wasn't at all as bad as my mother did, but it was how she started out. She found a way to let her anger out and from there became a monster like my father. I was not gonna let that happen to me.

After realizing that, I did whatever I could to not hurt my siblings. If I did hurt them I apologized right after. Holding my anger back from my siblings was causing me to backtalk so much more to my parents. That caused me to be in more trouble. I kept trying, but I felt like I was going to go crazy.

When I was 18, I realized another way to relieve my bottled up stress and anger was to hurt myself. That reduced my backtalk and reduced taking it out on my siblings. I would pinch myself hard, punch my throat, slam my hand on something really hard, and other things like that. It wasn't till I was 28 when I mostly stopped hurting myself. I completely stopped after we were rescued.

Watching my siblings wasn't all bad though. After a couple years, I realized that I could do things when my parents weren't home that made me happy. I had secret little concerts, I read them stories, we'd sing. We also had light up toys that I'd let them play with when the lights were off. I also didn't have to sit or stand constantly looking at a door or wall. And I didn't have to feel like a slave. I've always tried to find light anywhere I could.

4. HOPE

I had tried or thought I was trying to do the right thing here and there throughout life. When I was 16, I started a committed journey with God. It may have been very hard to keep my faith, but it was definitely worth every step.

When I was 16, I felt so lost. This couldn't be what God wants. I had depended on guidance from my parents. But I realized that I was looking in the wrong place for it. I wasn't sure what to do or where to start for good guidance. One night I had a nightmare that Jesus returned and I and a couple others were left behind. I cried in the dream and when I woke up I noticed I had actually been crying outside of the dream as well. I prayed for God to show or tell me what I needed to do.

I picked up my Bible the next day, and felt the urge to read it. I used all my free time to read my Bible. Everyday I prayed for God to guide me on what's right and wrong while reading the Bible. I read the entire Book within a few months.

I wrote songs, and used them as a part of daily worship and praise. Writing songs gave me a sense of freedom and happiness. I will tell my writing songs journey in another chapter.

When I was 17, I wrote a letter to God. I listed all I felt I had done wrong and asked him for forgiveness. I read that every single night in a prayer. I didn't know how to know if God had forgiven me. I didn't know back then that we know through faith. One day while I was singing my daily list of Christian songs, I felt an unexplainable peaceful presence rush over me. It felt like something completely cleansed my insides from head to toe. I instantly knew He was pleased with me.

My faith would waver, and other times it was strong. It was hard to keep it strong. I would feel God's presence which gave me peace. But, there were also times I didn't feel it at all and felt like He didn't care anymore. I felt like he left me in the midst of the darkness. My faith has been up and down so many times. At one point, I had almost lost any hope I had and almost gave up on God. But He was my only hope at all. So, even though I questioned Him, sometimes blamed Him, and wanted to stop the biggest war in my head, I held on to God. I would remind myself of the verses that say to walk by faith and that He will never leave us. And I am so glad I did. Each time I felt his presence leave, I held on, then when His presence returned my faith became stronger. It was a battle in itself to keep my faith and hope strong.

Probably the biggest war in my head was the one between right and wrong. The Bible tells us to obey our parents. If I obeyed them I hurt, and sometimes my siblings would hurt. Also that would mean that something as small as leaning against the wall was a sin because we weren't allowed to. Would that mean that I could never have happiness, because my parents seemed to try to drain every bit out of me. Do I listen to my parents or not? I wanted to give up and just simply do what made me happy, but I wanted more to hold onto my hope.

I also tried to keep all my stress, frustration, everything inside me. It would just bottle up, and I eventually explode on my siblings, my parents, or even nothing like staring at a wall while screaming and yelling everything. Sometimes I'd scream into a pillow, sometimes I'd throw something like my phone, and sometimes I'd hurt myself. I felt like I was going crazy.

I went back and forth so much. I would be on a doing good streak for weeks, then slip up and steal then lie about it. I kept trying though. I'd feel bad each time. But I seemed to be getting better and better each time. And I hoped that God could tell, I was at least trying.

My parents saw me reading the Bible. They saw me singing Christian songs. They knew I was writing Christian songs and excited for them to hear them. Instead of being happy and helping me do right, they called me a hypocrite. They would constantly say I was one. Eventually I started hiding that I was reading the Bible, singing, and writing songs.

Even with the bad, I held onto what I knew was true. I reminded myself that God's opinion of me is all that truly matters. And He knew I was trying.

Within the darkness, throughout life, God has done some pretty miraculous things for me and my family.

When I was 11, we were all in the van waiting for our mother to get something from a store. We were sitting in the parking lot when we noticed people looking into the sky scared. I couldn't see anything from my window. My father rolled his window down and looked over the van into the sky. He rolled his window up, looked scared, and just sat there. My mother came running out of the store. When she got into the van I found out what was happening. We took off as fast as we could. There was a tornado forming right above our van. It took my mother a while to get out of the store because they weren't allowing anyone to leave. On the way home, we saw many tornadoes forming in the sky. I saw at least 20, literally. I believe it was God who led us home safely.

When I was 17, I asked God to give me a dream of what Heaven is like, and He did! In the dream I felt God's presence strongly. I was in a wagon with an angel. I noticed on both sides of the road there were people tied up. I felt like that was symbolizing the people tied up in negativity and wrong doings who can't make it to Heaven. The angel was telling me about the events that were waiting in Heaven for me to do. When we reached the end of the road there was a gate, a huge gate. The gate opened and I went inside. It was so bright, but my eyes weren't hurting. I saw people, angels, and so many other things. I saw Jesus sitting with a bunch of children around Him. No words can describe how beautiful, awesome, and peaceful it was there. I kept thinking, "I hope this isn't a dream." I saw a girl run up to me. She acted like she knew me, like she'd been waiting for me. The weird thing was I knew her too! She was the first miscarriage, that I knew about, that my mother had. She wanted us to go talk to Jesus. As we started walking I woke up. I was so sad when I woke up. I wanted to stay in that amazing Place. It felt so real!

One night, I had turned all the lights off in our house. Mistakenly I did it in a way that I had to walk in the pitch dark to my room. I was barefoot, and there was trash everywhere including soda pop cans that were squashed and could cut my feet. I closed my eyes and decided to have faith I'd be ok. At that moment I literally felt someone take my hand and say, "I've got you". I walked to my bedroom safely. It felt like I was walking on paper plates the whole way. After reaching my room, I turned on my light and saw no one. I believe that hand was an angel.

Several times there'd be a fire on our property. I'd gather my siblings together. We'd pray and sing songs about faith. Each time the fire would go out, and we would be safe.

We heard on the weather radio that there was a huge storm headed our way. It was supposed to have golf ball sized hail, really strong winds, high chance of tornados, and lots of rain. I gathered my siblings and reminded them that if God can make the fires go away, He can make this storm go away. We prayed and sang songs about faith. After a while, I heard some wind. I looked out the window and the sky was pure grey, no blue at all. Not long after there was a sprinkle of rain. I just kept reminding myself and my siblings that God can do anything. The sprinkle stopped. I didn't hear anything. I looked outside and there was no cloud in sight. The sky was pure blue. There was also a double rainbow. In a matter of, no more than, 10 minutes the sky went from pure grey to pure blue. What was supposed to be a huge storm, ended up being a little sprinkle of rain. That had to have been God.

When we lived in the country, in Texas, the bathroom doors had locks. I had a copy of the keys. Twice I locked the key into the bathroom. The first time, I took a completely different key and prayed for it to unlock the door. It didn't. I kept trying for what seemed like forever. It was probably for about 30 minutes. Finally the key turned and the door was unlocked. The second time, I told myself, it worked before it'll work this time too. After about 15-20 minutes of praying and trying, it unlocked again.

In California, the pantry had a lock. I didn't have a key at all for that one. Our parents had left for a few days and told me that the pantry better not get locked. That if it does we won't have anything to eat. I was kind of in the habit of locking it. I accidently locked it and panicked. Me and two of my siblings tried to turn the knob. Then we tried using a card and then a knife. We couldn't figure out a way to open it. Then I remembered how God helped me with the bathroom in Texas. If He unlocked it with the key, He can unlock it without one. I put my hand on the knob, prayed, and on the first try it opened like it had been unlocked all along.

There were things God and Jesus did to remind me that They were there with me through everything. Here are two extraordinary things They did to show me I wasn't alone.

When I was 25, I had a dream that I saw Jesus! In the dream, I was in the dining room. I saw a Man sitting on the floor. I felt Jesus' presence strongly and wondered if it was Him sitting there. So, I decided to look at His hands to see if I could see His scars. As I reached my hand out toward His, He reached his hand up and our fingers touched. I was completely filled with a feeling that no words can explain. I could feel exactly how much love He has for me and all His power rush right through me! I completely understood how the woman in the Bible could be healed instantly just by touching His clothing. I woke up. As I was doing my morning singing to God and Jesus, I couldn't help thinking about that dream. The feeling I felt was so real. Did I really see Jesus, or was it just a dream? While I was singing, I heard Jesus say, "Reach out and touch Me." So, I reached my hand up toward Heaven. I literally felt a finger touch mine, and I felt the exact same thing as in my dream! The only difference was I was AWAKE that time! I knew I had actually seen Jesus!!! Later, I was watching videos online, and I found a video of a young girl who paints pictures of Heaven from visions she had. One of her paintings was a portrait of Jesus. The picture of Him looked exactly like He did in my dream!!!

When I would go into the bathroom, lock the door, cry, and pray Jesus would speak and comfort me. The first time this happened, when I bowed my head to pray, before saying anything, I was given a vision. I literally saw Jesus being beaten and laughed at while carrying His cross. The vision ended and Jesus said,"I understand." At that moment I realized, He doesn't just understand because He's all powerful and knows everything, It's more than that. He understands because He actually went through the same thing while on earth! After that everytime I went into the bathroom to cry and pray, He would speak to me and say, "I understand," "I've got You," "Trust Me," "You'll be ok," and other things like these.

Walk by faith, not by sight. He will never leave or forsake you. God and Jesus have proven this to me.

5. ABANDONED

When I was 18, my parents started leaving more often. They were also, quite often, gone all night. Slowly they were gone for 2-3 days, until they were eventually gone all the time.

The place we lived in during this time was a double wide trailer on the same property as the house we moved into when I was 11. And like the other places we lived in, it got filthy. Not only was there trash everywhere, there were kennels that stinked of dog stool and urine and trash that stinked of cat stool and urine.

My parents had gotten carried away buying dogs. They had bought about 8, and then some had puppies. We also had cats that had kittens. The dogs were mostly kept in the kennels, and the kennels were rarely cleaned out. The smell was everywhere. They were mostly let out to eat and drink, then had to go right back.

My mother would wake up in the middle of the night not being able to breathe. During the day, she had a hard time breathing at times. She had asthma and the stool and urine smell was affecting her badly.

When I noticed my parents leaving for a long period of time, I started begging her to clean almost everyday. I tried to get her to let me clean the kennels, but she refused to let me. She said the fumes would be too bad for me to breathe in. Umm, ok, wasn't I already breathing them in, daily?

According to my mother, they had to leave us, they had no choice. But according to me they did. They could've had me clean everything up or at least helped. We were all breathing those fumes in. They left us there to continue living in the fumes and filth. Or they could've left while I cleaned it up, but no that apparently wasn't an option to them.

Some good did come out of them leaving though. I watched movies that I wanted to watch. I listened to the radio a lot! I could dance and sing. I had little concerts of me singing my songs. I was able to get onto a good schedule of waking up early. I was able to freely do what I wanted and be who I wanted. My favorite thing to do was walk around the kitchen island, with the lights off, and sing out loud Christian songs. I wasn't in constant fear. So in a way, it was good they left us. But when I'd see headlights coming up the driveway fear struck my heart. I rushed to make everything seem normal.

I also taught myself to sing and dance during this time. There was a karaoke machine I hooked up to the television. I would sing hard songs to sing until I was able to sing it perfectly. I had to hold and hit all the notes correctly. I would turn the volume really loud to teach myself to sing loudly. I would watch music videos and copy all the dance moves until I had them down. I would then put all my learning into practice. I would turn the radio all the up. I would sing and dance to the songs it played. I would also make up dance moves. I wouldn't have gotten that opportunity if my parents hadn't left.

There was a big storm, I talk about in a previous chapter, that would've happened so differently if our parents didn't abandon us. Instead of a calm faith based experience, it would've been a fear filled one. Our parents would've most likely been panicking and have placed us all together. Their fear would've caused everyone else to fear. Or they would've placed us all in the van and drove off until the storm was over. Either way, we all would've missed out on an amazing miracle.

There was also bad to them leaving. My parents would drop off groceries about once a week, sometimes skipping a week.

We had to stretch that food to make it last. I would panic if someone got into something important or unfixable, like pictures or make up. I also put a stop to watching movies and shows I wasn't supposed to. So I tried stopping everyone else, which was stressful.

Overall I would say that my parents leaving may have been really bad, and they did not have to. But, for me it was kind of good. A lot less stress and a little freedom.

6. DEALING WITH SUICIDE

Starting at the age of 18, I had thoughts of suicide. I had them here and there up until we were rescued. Thankfully God stopped me from following through with it.

When I was 16, I had started trying to live for the Lord. I read my Bible asking God for guidance each day. I was constantly called a hypocrite by my parents. I was told so many times that everyone would be better off if I was never born. I would be told that things would be better if I just died. And that I was more than welcomed to walk out the door, but if I did I would never be welcomed back. If I had gotten something old to eat or drink, I'd be told, "I hope you die from that". I felt so unloved and unwanted.

After a while I started believing the things I was being told. I started believing that my parents would be much happier if I killed myself, that I was better off dead. They wouldn't have to see me or be ashamed of me anymore.

We were taught that if you kill yourself, you'd go to Hell. No one knows exactly what happens when we die. But believing that I'd go to Hell at the time, did not stop me from considering taking my life. I would think, "How can Hell be worse than this?"

When I was 18, there was a guy that my parents seemed to come close to setting me up with. I was a virgin. We were taught to remain one until marriage. This guy was the son of someone they knew. From what I was told about the guy, he was the party hard type. I was told by my parents that if they had me go with him, that they'd drop me off and pick me up later. They also told me that he'd most likely rape me if I didn't have sex with him. They told me to just let him do what he wants to me. Because most people that get raped will get killed so the rapist doesn't get caught. They said they would set it up. I prayed about it and thank God so much it didn't actually happen. But that made me feel so worthless, like I meant nothing to them. They were willing to throw me out and possibly destroy me.

I had different wars in my head that I just wanted to stop. I felt like I was going crazy. These are in no particular order. I had a war of right & wrong, a war of what I believe to be OCD, a war of trying not to become like my parents, and a war of everything bottled up inside & doing whatever I could to not explode.

The war of what's right and wrong was one of the biggest wars in my head. I have already mentioned it, but I'll mention it again. I have more to say on the subject. My parents made it close to impossible to "do the right thing". If we leaned on the wall we were sinning. If we threw our food away because we literally couldn't eat it, we were sinning. Also if I didn't tie someone up or do a punishment to someone that my parents told me to, I was sinning. I was torn. Do I do what I feel is right or do I obey my parents? Either way I was afraid I was sinning, because the Bible does say to obey them. But am I supposed to, even when I feel like they're wrong? It didn't help that I thought I had to be perfect to please God. That's what would run through my head pretty much everyday until God showed me, when I was 29, that I don't have to listen to them. That doing what I feel is right is most important. And that He doesn't expect perfection just our best.

The battle of OCD started as far as I remember. I think I was born with OCD, not sure though. Everything had to be in a particular order or in a proper place. When I cleaned I wasn't satisfied until I got every single spot I could see. When I did the dishes I had an order they had to be done in. It drove me crazy living in a home that was constantly a mess, knowing I couldn't do anything about it. I was called crazy and stupid by my parents for my OCD. I believed them, and tried to fix myself. I would force myself to not do things in a certain order. I'd try to think of excuses why I shouldn't be so much of a perfectionist. People who don't understand OCD, might not think of it as a big deal, but it was. When I learned, in a therapy group, that OCD is an actual thing and that I'm not crazy or messed up, I felt relieved. I still keep it under control. I won't allow it to control or get in the way of my life in any way. Also my OCD is not as bad as it was years ago. Now it's mostly that I have to do things in a certain order or a certain way.

My parents didn't believe in mental health. They didn't believe in OCD. I didn't even know it had a name until I was going to therapy.

One day, I heard someone mention on television a mental health problem. My parents started talking about a shirt they saw that mentioned a mental health condition. They said that things like that are excuses for people's behaviors. Then they mention that when I was little and going to school, I was diagnosed with ADHD. My mother looked at me and said, "You could've sat still in class and paid attention, right?" I said, "Right," out of fear. But honestly I didn't know the answer. Now that I understand it, I do have ADHD, and I do believe I had it as a child. Which explains so much! Like when I was told to check the temperature and a sibling said hi or asked a question, I'd completely forget what I was told to do. I got hit and called stupid and was told to pay attention. Moments like this happened so much!

Another war I had going on was to not become like my parents. I did everything I could to help my siblings and not hurt them. When I would hurt them, I felt bad. A lot of times, I'd hurt them by yelling at them and making them cry. I hated myself so much for that. I just kept trying to do what I could to help them. Over the years, I got better at not taking my anger, stress, and frustration out on them. I would keep that stuff bottled up inside, and then it would explode out of me. Sometimes in the form of me yelling, or throwing something like my phone, or hurting myself, or even screaming. I had to learn how to release the anger, stress, and frustration without me erupting like a volcano.

With these wars constantly in my head, everything being said to me, and the torture I was living through, I wanted to end my life and make it all stop. I felt like I was going to lose my mind and go crazy. If I did lose my mind, I was afraid I'd finally let my parents win and become like them. I would've rather died than allow that to happen.

I actually would come up with ways and plans that I could end my life. Some of my plans included drowning myself in the bathtub, stabbing myself, and sneaking my parents keys and sitting in a running car in the garage. When I would think about these things and plan to actually do one, I would interuptly think about my siblings and what killing myself might do to them. My parents might have wanted me dead, but I knew my siblings didn't. Remembering that, made me not follow through with doing anything.

I would however, do little things to feel something, anything. I was at a point I was numb. I couldn't feel much of anything so I would pinch myself, slam my hand on something hard, punch myself in the stomach or throat, and more. I would get laughed at by my siblings which only made me feel worse.

I also spent a lot of time in prayer about it. I didn't believe God wanted me to end my life. I kept having a dream almost every single night. I felt like God was telling me something. In the dream I was leaving my house, running away. It was short and simple. For about a full year, I had this dream. I would fill my backpack up, and make plans to leave. When I did that, the dream would stop. I'd change my mind because I didn't want to leave my siblings and dump my backpack out. Each time I did that, the dream would start again. After about a year, I finally decided to listen to God and leave.

7. MY ESCAPE

As you know from the previous chapter, I was having lots of thoughts on suicide. I was going through way too much and wanted it to all stop. I spent lots of time in prayer. I didn't believe God wanted me to end my life. I didn't know what to do. He gave me a dream almost every night showing me to run away. After about a year, when I was 20, I was convinced that was what God wanted me to do. So, I packed my backpack and took a shower. I left early in the morning as the sun was rising.

Before I left there were many times, out of frustration and anger, I'd yell, "I can't wait to get out of here." Some of my siblings would be hurt thinking I wanted out because of them. I would explain that it wasn't them, and I told them the reasons why and what our parents did to me. I'd get the reply, "They'd never do that, they love us." That would just make me more frustrated and feel more alone.

There was one sibling who stuck by me during this difficult time. They knew everything. I shared everything I was feeling. They knew about my suicide plans, me praying to God for help, and me running away. They helped me through that time, and I probably wouldn't be here if it weren't for them and their support.

I wrote a letter about how I was moving on my own and going to follow my heart and dreams. I rewrote it so much. The one I wanted to leave was so truthful, I was afraid that if I was found I'd be killed. I wanted to say exactly why I was leaving and what led up to that decision. Instead, I decided to leave the letter that was more hopeful simply saying I'm moving out. I did hope to make it on my own, but I knew so little about life beyond my home.

I had everything prepared the night before I left. Early the next morning, I got ready and left. One of my siblings was begging and crying for me not to go. But at this point, I felt like God really wanted me to go. No, I didn't want to leave my siblings. It broke my heart to leave them. But I was going to put God first and trust him.

We had kind of a long driveway from the trailer to the road. With each step I was afraid, but also felt kind of free. It kind of felt good to know I was leaving all that bad behind. At the time, the torture was mostly done to only me. So, I didn't feel like I was leaving my siblings to be tortured. I thought they would be ok without me.

When I reached the end of the driveway, I heard God's voice speak to me for the first time. Like, literally speak! After this experience I have continued to hear God speak to me. It is awesome! It's like a super loud thought. You really hear it, but others around you can't.

God told me to turn right, so I did. One of our dachshunds followed me. I tried to get him to go back home, but he wouldn't. After a while, I passed by a house that had a collie. The collie came running up to me barking and growling. The dachshund attacked the collie to save me. The collie and the dachshund were in a huge fight and I was screaming and crying. The guy who lived in the house ran out and called his dog. I made sure the dachshund was ok. I told him again to go home, but he refused. So, I kept walking.

When I reached the main road, a lady stopped her car and asked if I needed a ride. I told her I was fine, but then I heard God's voice again. He told me to get in. I was afraid, but I trusted God. I got into the car. The lady asked me where I needed to be dropped off at. I told her a specific store. On the way there she asked me questions. I was afraid to answer most of them. One of the questions she asked was my age. I told her I was 20. I knew I didn't look my age, so I told her I have my diploma to prove it. I didn't realize that a diploma doesn't prove anything. On top of that it was a homeschool one. So, that probably made me sound younger. After a while, she dropped me off at the place I asked her to.

I continued to walk. I saw some apartments and saw a guy outside. I walked up to him and asked if he worked there. He said he did. I asked how much an apartment cost. I don't remember the price, but I knew it was a lot. I asked if I could live there and when I get a job, pay back anything I owed. He said that I can't do that.

So, I kept walking. I didn't make a turn until God told me to. I completely allowed His voice to guide me. After a while, I saw a daycare. I was missing my siblings like crazy, and thought this would be the perfect place to work. I walked into the daycare, and asked to speak to someone about a job. There was a form I had to fill out. I didn't know my social security number, and I didn't have an address. I didn't even bring my phone. I asked if it was possible to work there without an address, They said no, that I have to have a mailing address. I told them I didn't know my social security number. They said I had to have it. I left feeling frustrated.

Apparently I was going to be homeless the rest of my life. I couldn't get an apartment without a job, and I couldn't get a job without somewhere to live. I just had to trust God, it's all I could do.

Eventually, I ended up on a back road. There weren't many people except for the cars passing by kind of fast. I sat down to rest. I tried to eat some chips, but I couldn't. I hadn't eaten anything all day, but I didn't feel like eating. I kept thinking about my siblings, and I couldn't get out of my head my sibling begging me not to go. I also kept remembering my mother saying that if I leave, I'll never be welcomed back. I started crying and again thinking about killing myself. I didn't want to feel any more pain. I stood up. As I made plans and prepared to jump in front of the next car that would rush by, God said, "Trust me." I moved away from the edge of the sidewalk and remembered, I have to trust in God's plan. I'll be ok.

I continued to walk, I crossed a bridge and went into a hospital for some water. I got some from a fountain, then continued on my way. I noticed a little house by a church. God told me to knock on the door. Again, afraid, I did as God said. I knocked on the door and a lady answered. She welcomed me inside, and I accepted.

She asked me some questions, most of which I didn't answer. I did have some pictures of my siblings I had taken with me. I couldn't stop thinking about them. I showed her the pictures. In those pictures you could see the filth on my siblings and in the house.

After her husband came home, they both talked. They were planning to go to a high school football game that night. They invited me along. We went to get pizza, but I barely ate anything. Then we went to the football game. They were surprised that I had never been to one. They explained what was happening in the game. It was actually fun.

When we returned to their home, it was time to go to bed. The husband and wife talked for quite a while. They allowed me to spend the night and gave me an electric blanket. I slept on the couch, and slept very well.

The next morning, God told me to call my mother. I was terrified and confused. But I did as He said. I asked to use their phone to call her. They said I could. I called, and when she answered I told her who I was. She was crying hard, and asked where I was. I wasn't sure but tried to explain kind of how I got there. She said that they were on their way.

My parents arrived and picked me up. While driving my mother kept apologizing. She kept saying she'll change and that she's sorry for anything she did. I believed her and was relieved.

When we reached our destination, I couldn't believe it. We parked in front of a motel. When we walked inside, it was obvious they had been living there!

As soon as the motel room was closed and locked, their attitude completely changed. Both of them were furious with me. They wanted to know exactly what happened. But the moment I mentioned that God told me to leave, I was apparently lying and going to Hell. They didn't change or treat me better, they actually got worse. I pretty much had to stay with them every minute that I could. I rarely got to see my siblings, the only reason I would've wanted to come back. I was a bad influence apparently, according to my parents.

Also, they tried making me feel bad about leaving my siblings. They mentioned me leaving my 16 year old brother in charge and me leaving was child neglect and they could have me arrested. Ok, lol, really? They had us both in charge, not me. And they are our parents, if anyone neglected the children, it was them. And, they had me in charge of watching my siblings, when they left to go shopping, when I was only 12! If anyone was at fault, it was them not me.

After a while we were banned from the motel. And had to find another one. We kind of bounced from one motel to another until they couldn't afford it. Then we were living and sleeping in the van. Until they finally found an extended stay motel they could live in. We stayed there until we moved out to California.

Looking back at it now, I believe God had me run away to give my parents a warning. If they didn't change something like this would happen. Did they listen? No, they did not. They only got worse throughout the years.

8. CALIFORNIA

1-The Good

When I was 21, I was told we were going to move to California. I didn't know if they were being mean and lying, or if we were actually going to move there. My parents knew how much I've always wanted to see California, where I was born. It was just like them to lie, get my hopes high, just to crush my happiness about it. They've done that quite a lot. They'd get my hopes high on something only to disappoint me and it not be true. So I didn't believe them until we actually started packing up for it.

I was so hopeful that maybe this move would change everything for the better. And at first things were good. We went out places more, we got to go to places like amusement parks, a new clean house, a fresh start. But, nope, I was wrong. Here is the good to us moving to California.

In the beginning of us living there, we got to play outside some. We got to use jump ropes and hula hoops and even got to run around. That stopped shortly after though. At the beginning of both cities we lived in, we got to eat outside. Again, that stopped shortly after. When we moved to Perris, the younger siblings got to go trick or treating.

We got to go to some fun places after moving there. We got a year pass to an amusement park. We went to the zoo. We went to Las Vegas, Arizona, and San Francisco. We also all went to the grocery store with my parents a few times.

We had family over a couple times. That was really fun. I

hadn't seen them in forever. Some of my siblings had never seen them.

I got my first smartphone, and started looking up songs and artists. Through that I realized how healing music can be, especially the songs I can relate to.

I had been writing songs since I was 14. When I was 9, I came up with a basic child's song for a make believe television show, not sure if that one counts. My first full length song, I was 14. I thought it was hard, and I thought I wasn't going to write another one. Well, when I was 16, I wrote another one. And from there, I just kept writing. When we moved to California, I was 21, and I realized how healing music can be, I started intentionally pouring my feelings into my songs. That was like talking to a really good friend. It was very helpful and made me feel better.

When I was 25, my father did something really bad that really hurt my mother. She confided in me. I will not go into detail because it is not my story to share. Almost every single thing I already knew. I had either seen it or heard it through their fighting. She asked me what to do, if she should leave him. I didn't know what to say. Of course I thought she should leave him. But a part of me was afraid that would be the "wrong" answer. So, I told her to do what she feels like she should do. During the small period, I felt close to her again. But, as soon as everything was ok between them, she went right back to being mean again. I had her back for a little bit, then she was gone again.

Some things were good, but things also got a lot worse.

2-How They Showed "Love"

My parents tortured and abused me, but they would've said they loved me even though they said I should die and go to Hell. They tried to show love by spending money on us. That's how my father tried to show love for my mother. He let her spend money on way too much, things she never used at all. They also tried that with us. Buying us stuff, or spending money on trips to places. They seemed to think using their money like that instead of what was important would show their love.

For Christmas we got crazy amounts of gifts. Some years we got 10 each, sometimes more! But some years one or some of us wouldn't receive Christmas as a punishment. These many gifts were not cheap either. They'd buy us nice things that would shortly be taken away.

After moving to California, we started taking trips and vacations. They bought year passes to an Amusement Park. We went pretty often. We went to Las Vegas which was fun. We mostly stayed in the hotel rooms while our parents went and had fun, but at least most of the usual torture wasn't there. So, that made it fun. We also went to Arizona and San Francisco, California.

In California I got to meet a celebrity. It was really cool, but I barely knew him. I was thankful and happy, but this person was more my parents' choice. My parents thought this was my first time seeing a celebrity. It was my first time meeting one, but not seeing one.

In Texas, I was taken to a honky tonk. I saw the first celebrity I knew. I had heard a lot of his songs on the radio, secretly. I couldn't act like I knew him out of fear of ruining the good moment. So, I kept my excitement inside. I did look at him though and smile, and he waved at me!

Although going out and going on trips was fun and nice, It had some big downsides. Everyone was led to believe that we were a perfect happy big family. It seemed like everyone believed that lie. We would take family pictures. And that would show us happy. We looked like the perfect example of a happy family. Yes, we were somewhat happy in that moment, but we were not a perfect happy family.

When I was 18, I "graduated". I didn't truly graduate. As I mentioned in an earlier chapter, I did not do much school. My parents ordered a homeschool diploma and took me to a graduation for homeschoolers. My mother gave a long speech on how proud she was of me. When we came home I had a graduation party with my parents and siblings. I had over $300 worth of gifts! Yes, I was happy I got the gifts and got to have a graduation. But I also was embarrassed being up there with the other people who probably did go through the full 12 years. Also while the party and gifts were nice, it was all a lie. I did not earn that diploma, I did not complete 12 years of school, and my parents were not proud of me. During that time they were still calling me a hypocrite and saying that everyone would be better off without me in their life. Saying that stuff shows they weren't proud of me, it was for show.

When we would eat basically the same thing over and over again, they tried showing love by getting pizza or fast food occasionally. Also they'd surprise us with frozen food here and there. They got that kind of food all the time. Real love would've been us always eating the same thing as my parents. Either they eat what we were eating or them giving us what they were eating all the time. They said they couldn't afford to feed us like they ate. I wonder why. It was all the money they had been spending on unimportant things; all the games, purses, clothes, dolls, etc. that we're barely touched.

If they wanted to show they loved us, they should have done it through actions, not through money. They should have acted like they loved us instead of acting like they wanted us dead. Things and money don't show love, caring and kindness do. They could've used that money to buy us food we could eat, and drinks other than unfiltered water, or even a filter for the unfiltered water.

I do appreciate the things I got to do. All the trips and places I got to see and have fun. But, that did not show love for me. And the memories are tainted with the bad memories tied to them.

3-The Bad

After the move to California, I was still being tortured. But the main torture was suddenly shifted to a different sibling. It's not my place to tell their story, so I won't.

I was still under a lot of torture, physically and mentally. But also everyone was. Everyone started being physically and mentally tortured. It was not mostly or just me anymore. From my perspective and what I saw, I was the only one tortured for many years by our parents. A few things did start happening to my other siblings, when we lived in the double wide trailer. But so much more was happening to me, I didn't see it. After moving to California, the abuse to my other siblings grew so much. Things were suddenly much worse.

When we would go out, it was nice. But it also had bad to it. My mother would brag about my age and size to people. That embarrassed me, especially when she'd do it in front of children much younger than me and bigger than me.

One time, we were at an Easter event at a mall. I was around 22, I think. In line, in front of us, was a mother and her 14 years old daughter. My mother starts talking to the other mother and gets on the subject of me and my age and size. The daughter was bigger than me. The daughter looked at me. She looked really hurt, which made me feel really hurt. In a way I felt like I was hurting her. I wasn't, but I couldn't help but feel like it. From then on, I hated my size so much. I wanted to be average size, but I was so underweight from malnutrition.

Also I had noticed some of my siblings comparing their size to mine. I told them I was just super underweight, to not compare themselves to me. I told them they looked better than I did. But they still compared. I believe it could've been because of the bragging they heard my mother doing about my size. But I don't really know. Either way, it wasn't good.

One of my most embarrassing moments happened because we rarely went out. I was asleep, and my mother woke me up. She said I could go to the grocery store with her. I was so surprised and happy. I jumped up and got dressed as fast as I could. While in the grocery store, I noticed people giving me dirty looks. I looked down at my clothes and noticed something horrific to me. I was wearing my filthy jeans! They were noticeably dirty and had holes in them. I am sure they stinked also. I could not wait to get out of that store and back home. I was so humiliated!

I hardly took showers. I only took them when I "had" to, like if I was going to go somewhere. And even then sometimes I didn't. Sometimes it would be months between showers, and sometimes years. My mother was in control of when we took them.

There were times I went months without brushing my teeth. But, there were times I brushed my teeth every night. Closer to when we were saved, I was brushing my teeth every night.

I basically wore the same thing all the time. Most of the time it was pajamas. Sometimes it was actual clothes. Those clothes became so filthy.

I became so filthy that you could literally scratch off the filth from my skin. I lived in filth and a horrible stench most of my life.

My parents had 3 favorites, the "good" ones. They were the ones we'd have to sneak past or make sure we didn't get caught by. Anything they spotted that would get us in trouble, they'd tell. By telling on us, they gained favor from our parents. They got to go out so much, they got to eat good food like our parents. They didn't get beat until they bled, or chained up.

I was considered a bad influence. I was a hypocrite. I was bad because I did what I felt was right. And I refused to become like my parents.

My mother seemed to be bipolar or something like it. One minute she'd be sweet and calm, the next she'd be yelling, throwing us across the room, and saying we should die.

I was afraid to ask even a simple question like how long to cook a microwave dinner that had options. She would either be nice and tell me, or she'd slap me, pull my hair, or hit me for being "stupid". I was to already know.

If I forgot what she told me to do, which was kinda often. I would get afraid to go ask her what it was I was supposed to do. My mind would drift off into thinking about something else causing me to forget what it was I was told to do. That made my mother very angry. I believe it was a part of my ADHD. She believed I was just being stupid and should pay attention.

A perfect example of her being bipolar or something like it, is this. I was making sure the girls brushed their teeth like every night. Usually everyone was made to be quiet. My mother yells for me, so I come. She tells me that it's ok for them to talk while I do the teeth that night. So, I let my sisters know. They were happy and everyone started talking. About 5 minutes after that, she yells for me again. I go in there and she pulls my hair and starts hitting my head yelling at me asking why they were talking. I told her that she said they could. She pushes me into the floor and yells that she would never say that.

When my oldest brother started going to school for his GED, I begged to get mine also. I knew they wouldn't let me, but I had to try. They said they thought about it, but decided not to. They said there was no reason because I didn't need college. I told them that I wanted to go to college. They said I was going to be a stay at home mom and have kids. I thought, "Who are they to plan my future! Yes, I wanted kids, but I also want a life for myself. I wanted a career!" I then tried the excuse, what if something was to happen to my future husband then I'd need that GED, college degree, and job. They just said that I should cross that bridge when I come to it.

At that point I knew I had to come up with a plan to get the life I wanted. I knew whoever I ended up marrying would be arranged by my parents. It had to have been, I didn't go out. And there was no way I would've had the chance to date. So, I planned that whoever I did marry, I would use them as support until I got my life together. I would go to college, get a career, and save up money. I also would have my own bank account and nothing tied to the guy. Then depending on how I feel about the guy, either stay with him or leave him. That was my plan and I'm so glad I didn't have to go that route.

We would have day shifts and night shifts so there was always someone on guard. We called it the day schedule and the night schedule. The day schedule usually started around 3:00pm-5:00pm and ended around 3:00am-6:00am. The night schedule usually started around 3:00am-4:00am and ended around 3:00pm-5:00pm. There were times I was on the night schedule, but was made to stay awake during the entire day as well. The most I was made to stay up was a little over 72 hours. There were reasons I liked the day shift better and reasons I liked the night shift better. Overall, the night shift reasons outweighed the day shift.

These are the reasons I liked the day shift. I got to spend more time with some siblings, secretly. I was able to sneak stuff to my siblings without getting full blame if something was missing. I didn't have to eat leftovers. And when my parents were gone, I could do what I wanted to make me happy.

Now for the reasons I liked the night shift. It was more daylight time. I got to see the sunrise. It was quiet. I didn't have my parents constantly yelling at me. A couple of my siblings would sneak into the kitchen with me. I may have had to be quiet but I got way more time to relax and be myself on the night shift.

I heard my parents fight way too much. I knew so much about them and their past through their fights. I had heard many times that I was my mothers biggest wish. To have a daughter to be friends with. I would've been that for her if she had just let me. When I was little, my father would do whatever he could to turn me away from her. He'd spend lots of time with me. He'd watch shows with me. He'd make jokes and make me laugh. He'd also give me sweet things like candy for breakfast, making my mother angry. I was my mother's light when she was good and being very abused by my father. He knew that.

During one fight, I heard something for the first time. My father did not deny it at all. He only confirmed it to be true. After I was born, my mother decided to leave my father. He found out, and threatened to kill me, a baby, if she ever attempted to leave again. That made her feel trapped. So, my father got what he wanted and she stayed.

That sent chills all through me. My own father threatened to kill me as a baby! His own baby girl! I mean they both threatened to kill me throughout life. But a baby!

I would also overhear many conversations they didn't know I heard. Every extreme punishment was my father's idea. My mother would fight it until she was convinced it was a "good" idea. But if he totally had it his way, every single one of us would've been tied up. That idea, my mother wouldn't be convinced until it was planned to move to Oklahoma. She agreed that once we moved there they would have every one of us chained up. At least that's what I heard.

I was really praying for a miracle even more than before. We had to get out before that happened!

9. STARVED

Up until our parents abandoned us, we ate pretty good. Except for the time I had to eat peanut butter sandwiches for a punishment and the time I had nothing but water for 3 days. We mostly ate 2 times a day instead of 3, but we ate. We also had a variety in what we ate.

When I was little, I remember my mother cooking a lot. I used to watch her and wish I could help her. Sometimes she'd make a birthday cake. That was fun. I'd watch her follow recipes. I would always get full when I ate. We would eat 3 times a day, but there were times we'd skip breakfast and eat twice.

When we moved to the country, I remember eating twice a day. At first there was quite a bit of cooking. After the house was trashed and became nests for snakes and mice, she stopped cooking. At that point we all lived in one room of the house. I was sent out of the "safe room" into the kitchen to prepare microwave foods or to get something from the refrigerator.

When I was 15, we moved into a trailer on the same property as the previous house. At first there was some actual cooking. Then soon after it was mostly microwavable meals. When we were abandoned, we were brought groceries about once a week. Sometimes, we'd skip a week, so we had to be smart on how to divide up the food. We never got full while our parents were away, unless we ate one big meal instead of 2 little meals.

When I was at the motels, I mostly ate one meal a day. At first I was eating twice. But then my mother got 2 jobs and my father still had his job, and I started eating once a day. I saw my father a little more than my mother. So it was him that would usually bring my food to me. It was mostly fast food, and pretty much on the way home from work. Even though I ate once, it was kind of nice being there alone. I missed my siblings like crazy. But in a way, I got a tiny taste of what it would be like to live on my own when they both were gone and at work. It was quiet and nice. But when they were at the motel, it was a different story.

When we moved to Murrieta California, the food started out good. There was cooking, fast food, and frozen food. Sometimes we'd get full, other times we didn't. But when we said we were hungry, we just got told, "You just ate." When I was about 23, my mother started doing some extreme couponing which didn't last long. We were stocked up on lots of food, mostly peanut butter. We had shelves full of peanut butter. We started eating peanut butter sandwiches and peanut butter and jelly sandwiches a lot. I liked peanut butter when I was little, but when I was fed peanut butter sandwiches as a punishment it made me hate peanut butter. Well, at this time, I was hating it even more.

When we moved to Perris California, we ate mostly sandwiches. It was mostly peanut butter sandwiches, some plain bologna or plain salami sandwiches, or a plain cheese sandwich. Sometimes other meats, but usually just that and bread. The meat and cheese sandwiches were treats to me until I got sick and tired of them as well. I got so sick of sandwiches that I literally couldn't eat them.

I would usually be told to eat plain bread if I couldn't eat the sandwich. I couldn't even eat that. I was sick and tired of sandwiches and bread. I couldn't eat white or wheat bread. The wheat was much worse than the white though. I would secretly throw away my sandwiches and bread. I would rather not eat than to puke. I knew puking would dehydrate you, and the sandwiches were at the point of making me puke.

Most of my meals, at that point, depended on God and a can

of soda pop. I would sneak a can of soda pop, open it slow and quiet or loud and super quick, and chug it. I would pray for that can of soda pop to be like a meal to me. I would open it loud and quick if the television was loud. Any other time I'd have to open it slow and quiet.

My parents would say they fed us. Why? Because, they allowed us to have like 3-5 sandwiches in one setting. They would also bring us, very rarely, fast food or frozen food. But we really weren't eating. I wasn't because I literally couldn't. But it felt good to eat the rarely bought foods I liked. That was so rare that it wasn't enough to make up for me starving and living off of soda.

Some of my siblings were like me. They literally couldn't eat the sandwiches anymore. If I wasn't going to eat it, I wasn't going to force them to. I secretly threw away theirs too. I would sneak our parents food, snacks, and drinks to them. At this point I was stealing to save our lives, to survive.

Our parents ate anything they wanted. They ate frozen foods or fast food anytime they wanted. I had to prepare their food when it wasn't fast food. It smelled so good. They claimed they couldn't afford to feed us the same as they ate. I believe that, but it's their own fault they couldn't. They tried to blame us. They said it was because we were stealing the food. If we were fed correctly, we wouldn't have been taking everything we could. Also if you can't afford it, then eat the same you're feeding us. Don't sit there glued to the television eating something delicious, while we're gagging on our sandwiches. The reason I say it's their fault for not being able to afford it is, they spent money on so many unimportant things. Clothes, expensive purses, movies, games (lots of games), and dolls for my mother. Most of the things were barely touched, some never messed with or used. It was totally wasted money that should and could have been used to better take care of us.

10. WHAT GOT ME THROUGH

As I was going through hell, I found things that kept me sane. Things that kept me going and somewhat happy. This is what got me through.

I spent so much time in prayer. I would ask for help, for comfort, and for a way out. I would run into the bathroom and lock the door, even though we weren't allowed to have it locked, to cry and pray. I would hear Jesus' voice and feel His presence. He'd assure me everything is in His hands, to trust Him.

I had 3 things from the Bible to help me. I would say them everyday and sometimes over and over. This is what it was...

Jesus will never leave you.
God will repay for you.
You will get your reward in Heaven.
Remember these 3. You will be stress free.

Remembering those helped a lot. I made a bookmark with that written on it, so I'd always be reminded. I would also remind myself that everything happens for a reason. I just need to walk by faith and not by sight. I have to trust God.

I would look for bright sides or light in any situation. It was very hard to find one at times, but when I would find one I'd hold onto it. For example, when I was starving, at least I was able to get something in me. If I was tied up, me and my siblings would have definitely starved to death. Also, any time I complained to myself about doing the teeth every night, or if I was stuck on the day shift, the bright side was at least I was able to see some of my siblings more often.

Being around my siblings was enough bright side for anything. They were bright lights in my darkness. We helped each other out so much. I was happy to be able to sneak them food, drinks, and snacks. I was happy to allow one hand secretly free when I was told to chain them up. I was happy to help them find ways to listen to music. It was stressful at times and sometimes I felt used, but I made this decision and no one was making me do it. I knew I could've been caught, but I was willing to help them and chance it. If I was caught I would have lost what little bit I had. I would've been chained up, beat, and would've lost my phone forever. But more importantly, I wouldn't have been able to help my siblings.

I also realized changing my perspective could help. Instead of being afraid and frustrated while sneaking food to my siblings, I turned my focus reminding myself why I was doing it. That helped me a lot. Not because I feel like I have to, but because I love them. I would also face the battle of right and wrong everyday. Was I sinning because I was stealing and loosening their chains? Or was I sinning if I didn't help them? Either way I was afraid I was sinning. So I chose to focus on the positive side of it all. I was helping them and making them happy. I would change my perspective on lots of things, this was just an example.

We'd also use each other kind of like therapists. Throughout life each of my siblings had been able to come to me, one on one secretly. I may not have been good at giving advice, but I was a good listener. I would sit there and listen. Sometimes one of my siblings allowed me to spill everything going on inside me. It was a good way for us to get stuff off our chest instead of holding it inside.

Music is a big thing that helped me get through everything.

Relatable songs, dancing, singing, and writing songs was a big help. Of course, I had to do any of that in secret. Writing songs was almost like talking or venting to a close friend you can trust.

I learned that drawing and coming up with different outfits gave me a sense of freedom. I could totally be myself when drawing an outfit that was all me.

At night, to calm myself into a nice sleep, I would imagine things and places. I would basically pretend something just using my thoughts, and I drift off to sleep. It would help me relax and to get away for a few minutes. I'd just have to fully ignore everything around me, clear my mind, and start imagining.

I had made up an entire world full of magic and adventure. I would go on pirate, mermaid, fairy, princess, and many more adventures. Just depending on how I felt and what type of fun I wanted to have. It would be so vivid, for a moment I'd actually feel as if I was somewhere else.

The most calming thing I would imagine was being a mermaid swimming in the ocean. At first I would be floating on a quiet ocean and feel the sun on me. Then when I was ready, I'd flip over and go into the ocean. I would have a dolphin friend named Shimmer and we'd go swimming. We'd explore the ocean, sometimes we'd explore shipwrecks. I would imagine the beautiful sea life. For a few minutes, I had peace, relaxfulness, freedom, and pure happiness. Sometimes I would get lucky and actually dream I was a mermaid when I fell asleep. Those dreams were the best! They felt so real too. I could feel the weight of my tail, the cool ocean, and feel everything around me. This is why I say I'm a mermaid at heart.

I had an imaginary friend named Crystal. She was a beautiful fashion fairy. I would visit her in my imagination and talk to her as if she was a big sister to me. We became very close friends. I met her mom, sisters, and friends. I would make up fairies with names and types, and I would draw them.

I know it wasn't real, but it felt real. Making it a perfect escape for when I needed it. And it was something my parents couldn't take away from me.

I would also use sleep as an escape. I would always try to get as much sleep as I could get away with. I was at a point where even my nightmares were better than real life. As a result I would get too much sleep. Sometimes I would lie and say I had a headache just to get in bed sooner, or at least try. My body was so confused when it came to sleep. On the day shift, I got too much. On the night shift, I got too little.

11. SPREADING GOD'S WORD

When I was about 22, me, a couple siblings, and my parents downloaded some social games. They were really fun. There was a bakery, a restaurant, a dragon isle, a house, a city, a zoo, and a farm all by the same makers. We were only allowed to play with each other. We were not allowed at all to talk with other people. We had a lot of fun playing together.

Each person had their own wall to write on. I started posting Bible verses on my own wall. My mother saw it and freaked out. She was so afraid of me getting into some kind of trouble. She told me she was proud of me for wanting to put verses up, but not to do it.

Something happened that I won't discuss because it's not my story. But, my parents deleted the games. All of them. I thought, this is my chance. Maybe I can start spreading Bible verses on other people's walls. I just wanted to spread God's love through Bible verses. But, it turned into something much more amazing.

When I was 23, I named my house Christian Love. On the house app, I started secretly posting Bible verses on each person's wall, at each place I visited. People started writing back on my wall, "thank you" and "I needed that today". That made me feel good. I felt like God wanted me to tell my story. So, I made a website and put my testimony on there. I did not tell the full story. I mostly put how I sinned and what I did wrong, the stealing, lying, and things like that. A little of my journey with God. He forgave me and performed miracles for me and my family. How I kept sliding into sin, but God forgave me each time. Trying to display God's love. I then posted my website on my wall in the app. People would read it and tell me it helped them and that it was inspirational. I was in awe. God was turning the bad into something more awesome than words can say.

People started asking me about topics in the Bible. They started having discussions about so many subjects. They would ask for verses on a particular topic, and I would gladly find the verses to give them. People started really looking up to me, trusting me. I had people telling me things like, "You strengthened my faith," and "I gave my heart to Jesus because of you." When they thanked me, I would tell them, "God is the One guiding me on all this. It's Him you need to thank." Before answering any questions, I would put the phone down and not pick it up until I felt God's presence. I learned a lot as well.

I met people from all over the world. Learned a little about different cultures. I also met people from many different religions. I also allowed them to speak first about how they feel and their beliefs. If they were willing to hear me, I was definitely going to hear them. I learned about, Catholic, Mormon, Jehovah Witness, Musilim, Buddhism, and maybe more I'm not thinking of. I also allowed an Atheist to explain her side and evolution. I treated everyone equally, and everyone saw that. I think that's one reason people liked me. I actually made friends with most of these people I talked to.

Also, I never pushed my beliefs on anyone. I simply offered to speak about it or help someone in any way I could. If someone didn't want verses on their wall, I would post something different on theirs. If someone didn't want to talk about it in any way, I simply backed off. I believe this is something we need to find for ourselves. It can not be forced. Pushing it on someone can push them away from it all together. So, I let people come to me.

When I was 24, I started doing the same in the fashion app. This was the greatest escape from my hell more than anything else. I felt the most happy when doing this. I helped so many people, and it was the most awesome experience and such an amazing feeling!

People would also ask for prayer requests. I would make sure to pray for each person and their needs. Because people can lie for attention, which did happen a few times, I was very careful how I prayed. I would pray that if the person was telling the truth to help them with _____.

By the time I was 25, I had over 800 neighbors in my house app and over 300 in my fashion app. Most of those people I helped in one way or another. I helped literally 100s of people with God's mighty help! There is no greater feeling than knowing that you're a part of something so big.

I started posting a few of my Christian songs. I put a link on my website. People seemed to really enjoy them.

My mother started talking about downloading the games again. I knew I would be in huge trouble for talking with people outside of us, for spreading God's Word so openly, for having a website, putting my songs online (which she didn't even know I wrote), and for making friends. I would've been mostly in trouble for making friends, I believe.

I let my fear do something I regretted so much. I posted on my wall and posted on everyone elses to read my wall. I told them that I have to leave the games. Then I deleted everything. All the games, my website, my songs, and a texting app I had so I had a better way to communicate with my friends.

After doing that, I felt so bad. I didn't know what I should do. I prayed that God would open that door again when I could freely spread His Word and Love again.

Thankfully, September 1, 2019, I was able to download those games again. I was very surprised that a few of my old neighbors still played. That was really cool. Now, God has revealed He has much bigger plans for me. I can't wait to see all He has planned for my life.

12. ANIMAL CRUELTY

My parents weren't only mean toward us, they were also mean towards animals. They beat, trapped, and killed them. They basically killed them. I already told the story of Smokey. Now, here are a few more ways they were cruel to animals and their stories.

When we had moved to the country, my parents had bought dogs to breed. These dogs were kept in cages. They only got out for bath time or for their kennels to be cleaned. When they were not in their cage, they were being held. No excuse at all, to me keeping an animal in a cage for a prolonged time is abuse. This was all the time.

When we moved into the trailer, on the same property as the previous house, my parents got really carried away buying dogs. They kept the dogs in their kennels all the time. The dogs only got out to eat, drink water, take a bath, or clean their kennel. After a while their kennel wasn't being cleaned. The dogs were living in their own filth. It stunk up the whole trailer.

One night, when my parents were gone, I was going to bed. I wasn't sure if they were coming home that night, and I was told to go to bed over the phone. As I walked into the living room, turning the lights off, our dog named Burrito looked at me very sadly. I felt as though she was asking me to let her out of her kennel. I wanted to, but I knew that if my parents came home, that I would've been in huge trouble for the dog being out. So, I went to bed. The next morning, Burrito was dead. I felt so bad and blamed myself. I should've let her out.

They eventually had all the dogs outside. Even when it was very cold outside, I mean below 32 degrees and occasionally under 0. These were tiny dogs; Yorkshire Terriers, Chihuahuas, and Dachshunds. One of the Yorkies literally froze to death one night. Her twin sister never left her side and died shortly after. We had a total of 3 Yorkies.

This story is kind of a long one. It's about the first animal I was so close to that I felt like he was my son. I was about 19. My parents brought home a tiny Yorkie that fit perfectly in one of my hands. I had decided that this little baby was mine, and named him Owen.

I had to secretly keep him as mine. And, we had so many animals that my parents said we could call them whatever we want.

Owen didn't have any teeth, so he couldn't eat dry food. My parents gave him mushy food. They said they were told to give him mushy food and gradually make it less and less mushy. So, they took dry food and let it soak in water until it was mushy. They did make it less and less mushy, but too quickly. They had given him dry food when he had only a few teeth. He couldn't eat that yet! He would sit by the food bowl and not eat. So, I secretly fed him mushy food. I very gradually made it less and less mushy, feeling his teeth along the way. After his teeth were all in I gave him dry food, and he ate it. If I didn't do that, he would've starved to death. I would've gotten in huge trouble for doing that, but I was not going to watch him die because of my parents' stupidity! So, I saved his life. During that, we grew a very strong bond. I felt like he was my son. I would secretly play with him. He was a huge light in my darkness. After I ran away when I was 20, Owen got very depressed. Over the phone I would tell him, "Mommy's coming home." He knew me as Mommy. I would try to make excuses to go back to the trailer, but I wasn't allowed to. I couldn't be "trusted". He passed away from what I believe was depression based on what one of my siblings told me over the phone. He was very depressed the whole time I was gone. He would stay to himself and never showed signs of happiness. He was also barely eating. I blamed myself for years. I felt like I had killed my baby. I was devastated.

At the time we were taught that animals don't have souls. If they don't have souls then they can't go to Heaven. I definitely hoped Owen was there. But I didn't think he was because of what we grew up hearing. I missed him with all my heart, and I couldn't forgive myself. When I was 22, I started asking God if animals go to Heaven. I was about 23 when He gave me a dream answering my question. In the dream I was high up, and God was beside me. I could feel God's presence, but I didn't see Him because I was just looking ahead. I could see Owen and the other abused animals we had, that had also passed away, playing and running around in beautiful green grass. They were so happy and free. I started crying and woke up. I woke up with tears running down my face. I was so happy that he and the others had finally found peace and were happy. I knew then that animals do move on to a more peaceful place. Only then could my own healing begin. I also very slowly began forgiving myself. I still miss my baby and always will. He will always be my first son.

When my parents got an animal and needed or "needed" to get rid of it, they would drive out in the middle of nowhere and drop it off at the side of the road. They did that with the animals that were still alive at the trailer before we moved to California.

When we moved to California my parents got 2 dogs. This story is actually about one of their puppies. Her name was Padme. She was so cute. She was made to stay in the bathtub and got hit if she tried to get out. This made her mean to anyone who hit her. I don't know who all hit her, but I know she growled and would try to bite my parents. She was nice to me and loved me. She would also get hit for growling. After a while, my parents decided to get rid of her. They said there was no way someone was gonna take a mean dog. So, they took that poor baby and dropped her off on the side of the road. Her "meanness" was my parents fault, not hers!!!

You may be wondering how this animal cruelty chapter applies to my story. I am strongly against animal abuse. Growing up watching these poor babies be tortured, tortured me!

13. THIS IS IT

When I was 29, my mother told me something that made me give up hope for her. I had made excuses for her through the years. But after this, I was done defending her.

My mother was recording a voicemail while I was doing dishes. After she had finished recording, she looked up at me. She said to me, "I always knew you'd grow up to be a slut and go to Hell. I've always known to watch you closely." Always? Like ever since I was little? That hurt almost like something stabbing me in the heart. Yes, she had said some really hurtful things in the past, but it was always out of anger. This time was different. She was in one of her good and calm moods.

"Going to Hell," hmm let's see. God has helped me through so many tough times. He speaks with me and comforts me. He has done many miracles for me. He has actually shown himself to me! I am NOT going to Hell.

"A slut?" Lol, really? I never even had the chance to be one. Does she even know what one is? I had never been with anyone in that way. So, she was not making any sense.

She has found reasons to call me a slut throughout my life. When I was 14, I was caught wearing a crop top my mother had never worn and her make up. Maybe she thought I looked slutty, but she didn't say that. No, she straight out called me a slut. When I was about 28, I took pictures of a couple siblings who were wearing towels. We were pretending the towels were dresses. We didn't have certain clothes of our own, so we'd pretend to have the outfits we wanted. In this case, towels were dresses. They were posing like models and I was the photographer. The picture was found and that's what my mother was referring to the day mentioned in the beginning of this chapter.

I was done. I would tell myself stuff to get me through the day. It felt like I was lying to myself. At that moment I knew I had been. I would tell myself, "She's only angry all the time because she's pregnant and stressed," "She's not looking over my shoulder to watch my every move to find a mistake, it's all in my head," and "She's only saying hurtful things because she's angry and don't actually mean it." I was right, I was lying to myself to make myself feel better. It did feel like she was always just trying to find a mistake in whatever I did. It felt like she actually meant the things she would tell me.

I tried to keep up hope that she would turn back to the mother she used to be. I wanted so bad to believe that. I hated the monster she had become, and wanted her to see what she was doing as wrong. But, she apparently never did. After her saying that in one of her good moods really opened my eyes. She was gone, completely gone. My parents hated who I was. They hated my love for music and singing. They also hated that I loved the idea of having friends and being social. It seemed like they hated everything about me.

I had to either hide while watching talent shows or fake a frown. If it looked like I was enjoying it, my parents would give me a look that instantly made my heart sink. Most of the time, while watching talent shows, my mother would have me do a bunch of random things like checking the house temperature, counting how many cans of soda pop there were, and things like that. They hated that I loved to sing and dreamed of one day singing on a stage.

They gave me so many lectures on things over and over again. The lectures were mostly on music related topics and sometimes on having friends. They would say the same things over and over.

The lectures on friends, I'm not sure when they exactly started, went like this. They would say that having friends is a bad thing, because no matter how much you trust or love them, they will most likely stab you in the back. They also said that they know for sure I would give into peer pressure, That I would easily be talked into doing something I wouldn't normally do.

When I was in 1st-3rd grade, there were these 2 girls who everyone wanted to be friends with. These girls automatically didn't like me, and it seemed like they tried turning the other kids against me. When I was in third grade, I was 9, those girls said they wanted to call a truce. That wasn't the exact words but basically what was said. They said they wanted me to be their friend, but I had to join some kind of club of theirs. At recess, one day, they were walking me to their secret spot. We passed a classmate of mine. He had freckles and the girls started laughing and making fun of him for his freckles. I got mad and stood up for him. They told me to be quiet and join them. They wanted me to be mean like them! I yelled at them defending the boy. They said I couldn't be a part of their club. I said, "Good, I don't want to be a part of your stupid club!" Then I sat down and comforted the boy. We became friends after that.

Ok, so what was that? I would give into peer pressure? At 9 years old I didn't. Yeah, I wanted to join their club and stop getting hurt by them. But I would've rather them continue to hurt me, than for me to be one of them.

Also, all the battles I was fighting in my head throughout life. If I did not give into my parents to become like them, I was not going to give into peer pressure.

Everything I am doing in life right now, is of my own doing. If I just think or feel like I'm being talked into something, I push away. I hate feeling trapped into doing something, so the second I start feeling a drop of that feeling I'm out of there.

The lectures on music started when I was, I think 21. I had told my parents, after finding out that auditions were going to start, that I wanted to audition for a singing talent show. They immediately shut that idea down and tried to crush that dream.

During the lectures they'd say fame is bad, that everyone who gets into fame goes to Hell, that fame will make me do bad and send me straight to Hell. They also said that lots of people end their life because they can't take the fame anymore.

Don't they believe I'm already going to Hell, that I should actually die and go there now. They've said it enough times. So in their eyes, what's the difference? And I've already experienced wanting to end my life because of my own parents. It didn't seem like there was much difference, except the fact I'd get to sing.

I had to keep my love for music and people a secret to try to avoid these lectures. I would listen to music, sing, and dance when my parents weren't around. I secretly would have friends on the social games mentioned in another chapter, before deleting the apps. I wrote songs but tried to keep them hidden. I was afraid that if they were found, that they'd be thrown away. So, I kept a copy of each song hidden in my email.

I felt like a caged animal. I was yelled at for the smallest thing. I was beat. I was only fed what was given to me. And, I was trapped, very trapped, literally and figuratively.

I wasn't allowed to walk around or get any type of exercise. I was mostly expected to sit and not talk. I would pace in circles and sometimes have an exercise list I would secretly do. If I was caught doing anything like these, I'd get in trouble. So, I mostly did it when my parents were gone or asleep. Most of the time I paced to music.

Throughout life I thought I hated myself. But after doing this, I realized I hated my life, not myself. When I was 28, I made a list of all the things I liked about myself, and I made a list of all the things I didn't like. I was surprised to see the list of things I didn't like was much shorter than the list of things I liked. I worked on each thing I didn't like one by one. And eventually became exactly who I want to be. It wasn't easy, but I did it. Instead of hating myself, I ended up loving myself.

From everything going on physically and mentally to not being able to be myself, I was done. I realized my mother was gone, and this torture was too much. So, when my sister asked for help in planning an escape, I gladly helped.

I was so proud of her for wanting to plan this. I had previously ran away and it ended up a failure. Nothing got better, just worse. And it meant a lot she wanted my help.

I helped for about 2 years. We considered many options, even running off during a vacation. I gave as much advice as I could, but I didn't know much myself. She had asked me for help because she knew I had left once. I helped however I could. I told her to get pictures for proof. That way whoever she talked to would be able to see she was telling the truth. I am so glad I told her that, because I found out later that the police were gonna bring her back home until they saw the pictures. It was when they saw them that they realized how serious the situation really was. She asked me to leave with her and another sister. I told her why I couldn't and she understood.

When I had left at the age of 20 and ended up back with my parents, things got worse. I knew if anyone left, my parents would lose more of their mind and things would get much worse. We didn't know if there would be an immediate reaction or a notice placed on the door. We just knew we had to try to get help. I knew I had to stay back to do whatever I could to help the ones still in the house, even if that meant me getting hurt more. Running away with her would give me a second chance at getting away, but I would've been left with tons of guilt. What if things went wrong?

I am so proud of my sister's bravery. I left once, I know the fear. The reason I didn't contact the police when I ran away is because I didn't even think to call them. I didn't know they could help. I was super naive and didn't know anything. Yes I was 20, but my mind was like a child's. I thought I was smart and mature. But in reality I knew nothing except that I had to get away from the hell I was living.

I was asked to be the one to call for my sister. But, my parents would've seen on the phone bill that my number made the call. They watched that closely or they lied to us, making us think that. So, instead I helped my sister plan to get our brother's deactivated phone.

I am so glad and thankful the police showed up quickly and everything happened suddenly. But I will tell that story in another chapter.

14. SURRENDER FROM WAR

When I was 29, right after new year's 2018, I finally had enough of the wars in my head, especially the one that was such a struggle on what is right and wrong.

I decided to fully do what made me sane and happy, to reduce stress and anxiety. I prayed and told God that I hope He understands. I told Him that I was going to keep stealing for me and my siblings, that was going to keep lying to protect myself and my siblings, I was going to keep listening to music even though I'm not allowed to, and that I'm going to stop listening to anything at all my parents have to say and do what I feel is good. I was very surprised that His presence didn't leave me.

A few days later, I prayed for everything to be totally in God's hands. I had been praying for an escape, praying for a way out or my mother to come to her senses. I was done praying for that. I started praying for everything to be left in God's hands. If this was the life He had for me then so be it, if not He'll get us out. I decided to completely trust in whatever present and future God had for me. No more praying for escape, just complete trust. It felt good.

I also decided to have a baptism, bringing in the new completely trusting God me and out with the struggling warfilled head me. I also knew that the Bible told us to get baptized and I was ready for it. I had no way to go to a church to get it done, so I asked Jesus to baptize me. I wrote out a prayer for before and during my baptism. I had to do it in the shower. One day, everyone was getting ready for the move to Oklahoma, so showers were being taken. So, I said the prayers and got baptized. After getting out of the water, I felt so good. Yeah, I felt good from the shower, but I felt so good inside. I knew God had accepted that as a proper baptism.

Here's the prayers,

Before Baptism
Lord, I ask You to stand by me and be the One to baptize me. Please make this water Holy if it needs to be. I really don't know how this works, but I do know that with faith and You this will be a proper baptism. I'm ready to be baptized in Jesus' name, Amen.

During Baptism
Lord, baptize me in the Father, the Son, and The Holy Ghost. I now come out new and cleansed in Jesus' name, Amen.

5 days after being baptized, we were rescued. It was when I let go of my fears, and put absolute complete trust in God that we were rescued. It shows me that leaving everything totally in His hands and giving Him complete control, is the best kind of faith we can have. It is hard to do but totally worth it.

15. RESCUED

We were about to move to Oklahoma. My father was just laid off of his job in California and got a position in Oklahoma. I mentioned this earlier, but the plan was for every single one of us to be tied up when we arrived there. If something didn't happen soon, we probably would've never been free.

On January 14th, 2018, around 2am, I was making sure the girls got their teeth brushed for bed. The very next morning we were going to head out for Oklahoma. Everyone finished brushing their teeth around 6:30ish in the morning.That was normal because we secretly were using that time to talk and help each other as we did each night. I went to bed, but not long after there was a knock on the door.

A sibling woke up my parents. They went to the door, looked out, and were discussing if they should open it. The knocking got harder. The people knocking said they were the police to open the door. I had very mixed feelings. Excited-Yes, the call was made and the police responded quickly. Scared-What's going to happen now? My parents decided to open the door.

The police wanted to come in, but my parents asked for a warrant. The police said they didn't need one and made their way in. There were several police. At least 5, I think there were about 8. Some stayed outside while others were in the house gathering everyone into the living room.

One police officer asked me where the keys were to the chains. As I left my bedroom to get the keys, I saw my parents getting arrested. My father looked completely angry, and my mother looked thoroughly confused. I had so many different emotions running through me seeing that. I was relieved that the situation was being taken care of. I was afraid that my parents might manipulate the police and we'd return to them. I was happy because things may finally get better. I was sad because no matter what they do, no one wants to see their parents arrested. I had anxiety not knowing what was going to happen next. And, I was worried. What was going to happen to my siblings? Were we going to get split up? Would I ever see them again? Would they be ok?

After I got the keys, the police officer had me sit in the living room with my siblings. After a while, he asked who the oldest was. I raised my hand. He said that he needed our 15 passenger van to drive us to the station, and that he needed my permission to drive it. I gave him permission and got the keys for him. We were loaded into the van and taken to the station.

I just kept reminding myself to walk by faith, not by sight. The fear of the unknown was very scary. I did not know what was going to happen, so I kept saying this verse to try and keep my faith up that everything was going to be ok.

At the police station, I was asked if I wanted to press charges against my parents. I was told that they only need one of us to press charges, and that things would be easier to move forward with. I said that I wanted to press charges.

We were all questioned about what happened. I was so afraid that somehow my parents could hear me. That made me so afraid to talk about what happened. They tried to assure me that they could not hear me. I pointed out that I could hear what my mother was saying in the room next to me. They told me that it was the camera room I was hearing. They said my mother was not close to me at all. I felt a little better, but I was still afraid they could hear me. After they were done talking with me, they sent me back to the room we were all placed in when we got there.

Before I went into the interview, all my siblings were there.

When I came back after the interview, the ones under 18 were gone. I thought they might've been in an interview, but asked an officer to be sure. I was told that they had been taken to a hospital to be checked up, and that we would be going to one also. I was very worried I'd never see my younger siblings again.

Me and my older siblings were admitted into the hospital after midnight on January 15th. We were in the emergency room first. They examined us and took care of us. Some people came in to take pictures of our bodies to use scars, bruises, or any other place as evidence. Later the same day, we were brought into a hospital room where all us older ones could be together.

It was very hard to sleep. I was so worried about my younger siblings. Falling asleep only gave me nightmares. Once, I woke up and our story was on the news. It was so weird. The news was talking about us. The next morning, the televisions were taken out of the room.

We were there for 2-3 months. It felt way longer. Yes, I guess we were still kind of trapped, but to me I felt so free. No abuse, I could be myself, I wasn't living in constant fear. I had nightmares every night because of the hell I just got out of and the fear of what's going to happen with my siblings. Were they ok? But, still I felt freer than I ever had.

After our time in the hospital, me and my older siblings moved into a nice house. We lived there for about a year. It had its good and bad times, but overall it was really nice. And we were able to visit with our younger siblings. Life was far different, but much better.

16. MY STATEMENT

My parents' sentencing was coming up, and I was nervous. I had the option of speaking at it or not. I didn't know what I should do, so I prayed for God to guide me. I decided to write out what I wanted to say. I knew if I did go, I wouldn't have been able to think clearly. So, I wrote my statement down, prayed for God's guidance on that too, and looked over it many times until it was perfect. I didn't know for sure until the day of if I was going to speak or not.

While all this was on my mind, I was not all happy and bubbly like everyone was used to seeing me. I went to my therapy group place and one of my close friends noticed something was wrong and asked me about it. This was before I was allowed to tell anyone who I was. So, I told him that I was ok. He knew something was wrong, so he asked again. I knew I needed to talk to someone, and he was offering his help. I was sure it would be safe to tell him. So, we went into a room where just me and him could talk. I told him who I was and what was about to happen. That there was a big chance that I would be speaking, but terrified to see my parents. He was very understanding, and He offered to be there by my side as I speak, if I speak. I told him I would highly appreciate it.

When the court day came around, me and one of my siblings were escorted into the courtroom through the back of the courthouse, away from the media. We went up to a room to wait. 2 of my friends from church showed up. I told my lawyers and conservator that my friend was coming. Thankfully I didn't get lectured about him knowing who I was. I was glad he was welcomed in. I was relieved when he showed up.

When we walked into the courtroom, I saw my father first. He looked so angry. I had fear run all through me. I saw my mother next, she looked happy to see me, which was a little confusing. I tried not looking at them. I have very little memory of what was said in court, my mind was too full of thoughts, memories, and feelings. I just wanted to get this over with. I was told, by someone beside me, that it was my turn to speak. I shakily placed my paper on the desk type thing in front of me. My friend stood beside me. I had a hard time starting. I felt frozen. I felt like I was going to cry. I could hardly breathe. But I took a breath, within me said "God help me", and read my statement.

I said,
"My parents took my whole life from me. But, now I'm taking my life back. I'm in college now and living independently. I love hanging out with my friends, and life is great. I believe everything happens for a reason. Life may have been bad, but it made me strong. I fought to become the person I am. I saw my dad change my mom. They almost changed me, but I realized what was happening. I immediately did what I could to not become like that. I'm a fighter, I'm strong, and I'm shooting through life like a rocket."

I sat back down, and tried to breathe. I could not think or pay attention. I did hear all the statements, including my parents'. My father's was not sincere at all. I thought my mother's might have been sincere, but was also afraid it was only blind hope. I do hope she realizes exactly what she's done and gets help to better herself.

After what seemed like forever, we were escorted out of the courtroom. I was so relieved that it was over. I am very glad I spoke up, it felt good to say what I needed everyone to hear. I thanked my friends for being there to support me. I believe it would've been much worse if they weren't there. And it meant the world to me. But more importantly, I could not have done that at all without

God's help.

17. MY LIFE NOW

The life I have now is full of so many blessings. I am very happy and doing much better. Life is awesome. I wouldn't have been able to get to where I am now without God. I have learned to always put God first in my life. He has opened so many doors for me.

After finding a church I could call home, I have been truly blessed through it. I truly believe God has led me there. I started going, I believe in August 2018. I think it was in November 2018 that I started going to the Spanish sermon.

I have always had the desire to speak Spanish. I always thought it was a beautiful language. I figured going to the Spanish sermon would help me learn. It was so nice and beautiful. I loved it so much. I caught some words here and there, but they were being said so fast it was hard to comprehend.

In December 2018, I was in one of the Spanish sermons, something big happened. It was the last week in December. During the worship music, God spoke to me. He let me know that the reason I have a desire to learn spanish is that He is planning to use that in my future.

He also told me that what I had done in the social games, a few years back, was just the tip of the iceberg! If you look at a picture of an iceberg, it is just the tip that's above the water. Underneath the water is a much bigger part of the iceberg. I had helped hundreds on those games. If that is just the tip, what was He planning? Thousands? More? I started crying because what I did know is that He was planning something very big for my future.

They were celebrating the turning of the new year, that day, with spontaneous baptisms. I felt a tug from God to do it. So, I did. I looked at the pastor's wife beside me, and asked her to baptize me. It was a truly blessed and awesome day!

Ever since that day, He has very slowly revealed to me His plan. He plans to use my story of the hell I went through and turn it into something so beautiful. I have been led by Him to write this book, tell my story of the hell I went through and how God helped me through it and out of it.

I wasn't sure about how I'd go about doing it. But I knew that if it was God's plan, the doors would open up. So, I just left it in God's hands and thought about it. About mid 2020, I was ready to start working on writing a book. I was sure it was God's plan. As soon as I was sure of this, my eyes were opened. This is what He meant! This book will help far more than the hundreds that I have previously helped. I was overwhelmed with so much joy. There is no greater feeling than knowing God is using you for something this big.

I went through a continuation school and got my GED. Then I went through college and graduated from 2 different schools.

I am now a phlebotomist and absolutely love my job. I have a driver's license and vehicle. I am free and on my own to live my life. I'm doing things I've always wanted to but never could. And even though my parents told me I wouldn't make it on my own, I am.

I am living the life I have always wanted. I have good friends, have a driver's license and vehicle , have a career, and live independently. I also have started a business selling fashion accessories.

I have a cat. It scares me because he is the 2nd animal, out of many animals I've gotten so close to, that I feel a super strong bond to. Owen was my first son, this cat is my second son. Here's his story.

I went to an animal shelter to get a kitten. I thought I was going to get a female black kitten and name her midnight. I was wrong. When we arrived at the shelter, my friend found a female black kitten. I looked back at the kitties. All but one was playing and running around. The one that wasn't playing, was a male grey kitten. He was sitting on a post staring at me. I said, "Ok, I'll pick you up." As soon as I picked him up there was an instant connection. The connection reminded me of my original Smokey. I knew he was the one, and I knew his name. I told my friend to put the black kitten down. I told her I found the one I want, and his name is Smokey Jr.. So, many times I look at him and say, "Thank you for choosing me to be your mama." And, yes, I spoil him.

He is now officially my emotional support animal. He has his own ID card and ESA tag. He knows when I'm upset and knows how to make me smile. He comforts me so much.

I don't have any contact with my parents, and I never will. Even if they completely changed and I knew it to be 100% true, I don't think I could let them into my life. I have PTSD from the hell they put me through. Seeing my parents, during the sentencing, made it flare up more than anything else does. I would be strongly dealing with it on a daily basis if I let them into my life. And I'd be in constant fear of their manipulation. I need to take care of myself.

I've known from the beginning of our rescue I was never letting my father back into my life. But I struggled and went back and forth on the decision about my mother. I still had the hope that she would divorce my father, completely cut him off, and better herself. It wasn't until I was 32, I fully came to the decision to never allow her in my life either.

After her sentencing speech I decided to give her one more chance. One of my siblings who was in contact with her told me enough stuff that I realized there was no hope for her. She saw my sister's and my documentary and of course made it all about her, acting as if we were lying. She's manipulating the system to shorten her sentence! And she isn't admitting to anything she's done. More recently I listened to a podcast she was on. She basically blamed my father for everything and took no blame for herself! Yes he was the mastermind behind it, but she is very much responsible for her own actions. How can you be sorry for something you won't even admit you did? She's not sorry. She hasn't changed. And I am done having hope for her and allowing her to hurt me with that realization. She's on her own, and so is anyone who has sided with her or my father!

Do I forgive them? There's times I believe I do, but then there are times during a PTSD moment I literally hate them. So not sure if I have fully or ever will. It took a long time, but with God's help I have finally gotten this far. That does not mean I have to let them back into my life. That also does not mean I ever have to see them again. The healing and forgiveness process only started once I had disowned them as my parents. To me they're just two people in this world who really messed up. I have a hard time calling them my parents. I can't call them by their first name either. So I simply called them D and L, just the first letter of their name.

I used the words parents, father, and mother for the sake of the book. So everyone would know who I was talking about without confusion.

CONCLUSION

Life is awesome now. I'm telling my story to help people in any way I can. I want people to not feel alone, to know there's a light at the end of that very dark scary tunnel you're walking through. It is impossible for me to exactly show or tell you how bad everything really was. I feel like the words in this book aren't quite enough to convey what I was feeling through all of that.

I would love to see a law placed that makes homeschoolers and private schools do their job. There should be random check-ins to make sure the area is good and clean. To make sure the children look healthy. And to make sure they are being properly taught what they should know. Any signs of abuse should be looked into.

If you hear anything suspicious from a neighbor like yelling, screaming, anything at all that's suspicious, please have it checked out! It's not gonna hurt anything if there's nothing to hide.

Say something, do something! Don't just say, "It's none of my business." There could be a child being hurt, abused in any number of different ways. Abusers are gonna be good at hiding the abuse. They're not gonna want to get caught. I know mine were awesome at making people believe they were great people and parents. They fooled some family members and their friends into believing everything was good. As for bruises and cuts, they told everyone we just play rough.

Also for those still stuck in situations similar to mine. Find a way out. You're stronger and braver than you know. But before going to the police or any one that may be able to help, get pictures or proof. Make sure you have evidence to back up what you're saying. It sends chills through me knowing that if my sister didn't have the pictures I told her she needed, we'd all be in Oklahoma right now chained up. And life would have gotten worse.

God was there through the hell I was living, helping me. Even if it seems like He doesn't care, He does. My life made me stronger in faith. If God can help me through and out of this, I know He will help you through whatever you're going through. Sometimes I felt him, but there were times I didn't. It felt like He had left, like He didn't care. But, I would remind myself what the Bible says, and I walked by faith the best I could. When I look back on the times it felt like He left I realize, He was taking a step back for me to grow and become stronger.

The biggest thing I think I've learned on my journey with God is to have complete faith. Completely leave everything in His hands. I don't usually pray for things. I pray for everything to happen according to God's will. Things turn out so much better when we completely trust in Him and His plan.

I use my past to be thankful for the present. If anything bad comes up in my life, I remind myself of my hellish past. Nothing can be worse than living my entire life in torture. That makes my bad days turn into good ones. It also helps remind me to be thankful for everything in my life now. There was a time when none of what I'm doing now was possible, even something as small as going for a walk. I also choose to focus on the positive in life and weed out the negative.

My parents didn't necessarily raise me, God did. I fought to not become like my parents, and I held onto the Bible and God's guidance on everything. When I opened my Bible at the age of 16 to start my amazing journey with God, I asked for His guidance and to give me wisdom to know right from wrong. I learned just what a loving God He is. The person I am today is because I put my trust in God even through the darkest times. He taught me how to be a good person, how to love, how to be strong, how to be successful, how to be resilient, and so much more. He taught me what real love is.

I believe God has a plan for us and allows us to write our own story, as long as it aligns with His will. But, darkness tries to destroy any happiness God brings. It's up to us as God's children and warriors to push through the bad and see God's goodness and grace.

God did not make my parents bad. God is only good and love. Darkness got a hold of them and planted the idea of wrong. When darkness tries to tempt us or tries to make us do wrong, it's up to us to push it away and say no. It's up to us to do the right thing. God is not to blame for the bad that happens to us. So, where was God? He was right beside me. He was watching over me. And, Jesus was holding my hand through it all.

(Newborn picture
07/28/1988
Whittier CA

running into my
paternal grandparents
home excitedly
(4 years)

04/16/1996
School pic ♡ ↗

18 years old
Fake graduation ↗

The circled puppy was Padme. The rest of the puppies were sold. Padme was cruelly abused. ♡

Me not long after moving to California

Me sneaking and dressing up while our parents were gone shopping.

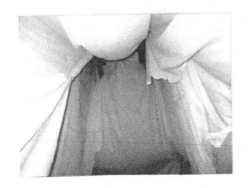

Fun in the hospital!

The nurses did what they could to make us happy and comfortable♡

Being silly in my therapy place ♡

When I first got Smokey Jr. (2 months old)

My GED graduation

My First Car ♡

First Day of
My Medical
Assistant Classes

Graduation
Party Photo
For My
Phlebotomy
Class

Made in United States
Orlando, FL
28 October 2024

53198125R00055